D1737521

POSTTRAUMATIC STRESS DISORDER

... Additional Perspectives

MERRILL I. LIPTON, M.D.

In the Private Practice of Psychiatry
Retired from the Veterans Administration

Former Academic Appointments:
Jefferson Medical College
Temple University School of Medicine
Texas A&M University School of Medicine
University of Pennsylvania Graduate School of Medicine

CHARLES C THOMAS • PUBLISHER
Springfield • Illinois • U.S.A.

Published and Distributed Throughout the World by

CHARLES C THOMAS • PUBLISHER
2600 South First Street
Springfield, Illinois 62794-9265

© *1994 by* CHARLES C THOMAS • PUBLISHER

ISBN 0-398-05899-7

Library of Congress Catalog Card Number: 93-37142

With THOMAS BOOKS *careful attention is given to all details of manufacturing
and design. It is the Publisher's desire to present books that are satisfactory as to
their physical qualities and artistic possibilities and appropriate for their particular
use.* THOMAS BOOKS *will be true to those laws of quality that assure a good
name and good will.*

Printed in the United States of America
SC-R-3

Library of Congress Cataloging-in-Publication Data

Lipton, Merrill I.
　　Posttraumatic stress disorder — additional perspectives / Merrill
I. Lipton.
　　　　p.　　cm.
　　Includes bibliographical references and index.
　　ISBN 0-398-05899-7
　　1. Post-traumatic stress disorder.　I. Title.
RC552.P67L57　　1994
616.85'21 — dc20　　　　　　　　　　　　　　　　93-37142
　　　　　　　　　　　　　　　　　　　　　　　　　　　　　CIP

PREFACE

This book was written to share extensive and unique experience with posttraumatic stress disorder (referred to as *PTSD*). The experience started in military combat in Europe during World War II, when at age twenty my body was shattered by the close explosion of a large artillery shell, and I was left for dead on the battlefield, with serious injuries from head to toe. After spending two years in army hospitals, I was suffering from distressing and often disabling symptoms of PTSD that nobody understood at the time. Typical for the era, I felt ashamed, unable to talk to anyone about the problems, and thought I was the only one so afflicted. This lowered my self-esteem and confidence and served to intensify the painful distress. Fortunately, with time and by trial and error, I gradually developed some understanding and learned techniques that improved my condition. Since then, I have always tried to use personal memories and experiences to better understand and help others with similar problems. The fact that I spent so much time as a patient enables me to relate to the feelings of all patients.

When in 1980 the diagnosis of PTSD was established in *DSM-III (The Diagnostic and Statistical Manual of Mental Disorders-Third Edition)*, I was enthused and started using the information to help patients. I was working in a Veterans Administration Medical Center at the time, and in 1981 started a PTSD treatment program that included group therapy, individual therapy, family therapy, and medication.

During the early years of this treatment program, the diagnosis of PTSD related exclusively to wartime trauma in military combat and as a POW. Other causes of the disorder were not considered. As time went by, however, additional causes became apparent. My first example was a veteran who did not see actual combat, but worked in a graves registration unit, picking up bodies and body parts. He was able to fit comfortably into the PTSD group, since he suffered from similar symptoms and problems. It gradually became obvious that symptoms of PTSD can result from a multitude of traumatic life experiences, not just war.

Over the years I have become aware of some special problems in dealing with PTSD. One serious problem is that the diagnosis is usually missed. Therefore, the ways and reasons why people deny and cover up symptoms of PTSD are reviewed and discussed, along with clues to the diagnosis. I still often see patients with PTSD who have been treated by various therapists over the years for anxiety, depression, substance abuse, or psychosomatic symptoms. Many of these patients had severe childhood trauma, sometimes a multitude of traumas. They are surprised when I ask them about their trauma and make the diagnosis of PTSD. They usually say they never told anyone about it before, that past therapists never asked them about trauma, and they did not volunteer the information.

Children frequently suffer from symptoms of PTSD that are misdiagnosed or not diagnosed at all. Childhood trauma, all too common in these turbulent times, is increasing the numbers of children suffering from this disorder who need proper diagnosis before they can be helped. These children are called hyperactive, are often labeled as troublemakers, or given the diagnosis of Attention-Deficit Hyperactivity Disorder.

When the diagnosis is missed, treatment for the underlying problem (PTSD) is not an option, and is therefore unavailable. Unfortunately, there are relatively few therapists who have training and experience in evaluation and treatment of PTSD. I sincerely hope that health professionals will correctly identify PTSD more often after reading this book, and feel more competent to treat it effectively.

ACKNOWLEDGMENTS

I am indebted to many people for my knowledge and understanding of PTSD. Since I learned most from my patients, I want to express my appreciation to all of them.

John Romano, M.D., was chairman of the Department of Psychiatry of The University of Rochester School of Medicine when I entered in 1947. This scholarly and charismatic physician was truly inspirational, and deserves the credit for my decision to go into psychiatry. Many other members of my class also went into psychiatry. He told us as first year medical students that psychiatry was ninety percent common sense (he now says ninety-five percent). That has always stayed with me, and enabled me to use common sense in dealing with treatment problems. This made possible many of the innovative ideas described in this book.

I must also express appreciation to The Veterans Administration. Since they authorized me to spend time treating veterans suffering from PTSD, I was able to learn and gain valuable experience.

I also want to express appreciation to William R. Schaffer, PhD, ACSW. He and I were cotherapists and ran the PTSD program together at the VA Mental Hygiene Clinic from 1981 through September 1987 when I retired.

I particularly want to express appreciation to my wife, Elaine. Without her help and support in so many ways, this book would never have been written.

My son, Dennis, did most of the typing and editing, and he did a great job. I also appreciate my daughter, Cheryl, for a lot of good work on editing and typing before Dennis could become involved.

INTRODUCTION

In recent years it has been more often recognized that posttraumatic stress disorder may result from physical and sexual abuse, auto accidents, war, rape, natural disasters like storms and earthquakes, and other obvious trauma. However, PTSD can be caused by a wide diversity of traumas that are often overlooked. Some examples include experiences that at some level are perceived as a threat to life, such as passing a highway accident where someone lies injured or dead, or realizing that something was just swallowed that is potentially harmful. Accidental injury to self or someone else at home or at work, or a near accident while driving are examples. It could be the witnessing of a store robbery, a highway accident, or other violent or potentially violent situation. Wives of servicemen alerted for combat assignment can start having vivid thoughts, ruminations and nightmares of their husbands being killed violently in combat, and other symptoms of PTSD, even before their husbands leave home. I keep finding PTSD in a surprisingly large number of adults who were subjected to abuse during childhood. The simple fact is that PTSD is far more common than formerly suspected, and needs to be identified more consistently so that appropriate treatment can be offered. A large section of this book is therefore devoted to accurate diagnosis.

In the past, when speaking to professionals about PTSD, I found that relating my personal experience to a particular symptom or issue was helpful and was appreciated. In addition, patients suffering from PTSD feel more comfortable admitting to their symptoms and emotions when they know that I have been through similar experiences. I also prefer to use myself as an example of a particular problem, rather than using one of my former patients as the example. In this book I therefore include personal experiences whenever I feel it will help the reader relate to a problem or symptom.

The book was written primarily for physicians and other professionals involved with the identification and treatment of PTSD. Other professionals may include nurses, psychologists, social workers, counselors including pastoral and school counselors, and students in these various professions. In addition, since I write without the use of technical terminology and jargon, the book can be helpful to many in the general public, including patients who suffer from PTSD and wish to understand more about their condition and treatment.

The book is divided into five sections. The first section includes a brief relevant history of PTSD and a review of issues and considerations that can be helpful in understanding, evaluating, and treating PTSD. This is relevant because we all grow up with culturally determined attitudes about the issues. For example, culturally determined attitudes continue to influence patients to avoid treatment because they feel ashamed of having problems.

The second section includes a listing of each symptom in *DSM-III-R*. Each symptom is a chapter heading and is fully described and discussed, using information gained from evaluating and treating hundreds of patients with PTSD since 1981. Much of this information has never before been published. Symptoms are described in a way that suggests appropriate treatment strategies. Nineteen additional symptoms also associated with PTSD and not listed in *DSM-III-R* are then described. Some symptoms are unique to PTSD and can be helpful in making the correct diagnosis. The symptom of *ruminations,* or the reliving of a traumatic event, is described as the central symptom of PTSD that has important implications for treatment.

The third section is a review of prevention of PTSD. Guidelines to prevent the development of symptoms following trauma are discussed. A number of specific recommendations are made that can help deal with this important public health problem.

The fourth section presents a review of treatment. It includes considerations in planning treatment, goals of treatment, helpful suggestions for treatment, and modalities of treatment. An innovative type of group therapy is described that has been most successful. Treatment of acute symptoms is reviewed. Then each symptom and its treatment is a chapter in itself, with many specifics provided. The treatment section also includes chapters on medication and on duration of treatment.

The fifth section has chapters on special considerations with combat veterans, legal considerations, and recommendations for dealing with disasters.

The reader will notice repetition throughout the book. This was done because many problems and issues apply in two or more symptoms or situations. I would rather repeat a particular consideration in the new context, rather than assume that everyone remembers from another part of the book and knows how it fits into the new context.

This book introduces some innovative and important departures in diagnosis and treatment. For instance, time spent reliving traumatic experiences is viewed as the central core of PTSD, since a past episode is relived with the full emotional intensity of the original event. The individual can therefore be retraumatized many times daily, with intensity of the experience undiminished over the years. Triggers that start such a disturbing experience are therefore best avoided. The described treatment program helps the patient gradually reduce total daily time spent reliving traumatic experiences. The concept of total daily time spent with ruminations is another innovative aspect of treatment that helps patients learn to gradually reduce symptoms and better cope with their problems. During treatment, therefore, discussion of the individual's traumatic event is avoided as much as possible so that triggers are kept to a minimum. This approach to treatment is supported by recent findings in neurobiology indicating the need to reduce alarm responses. The approach is in contrast to the usual treatment in which past trauma is often the focus of discussion.

CONTENTS

SECTION III: PREVENTION

SECTION IV: TREATMENT

SECTION V: ADDITIONAL CONSIDERATIONS

POSTTRAUMATIC
STRESS DISORDER
. . . Additional Perspectives

SECTION I
PERSPECTIVE

This section provides a brief background and framework for understanding the development and treatment of posttraumatic stress disorder. In Chapter 1, the history of PTSD is discussed. Chapter 2 is devoted to the understanding of PTSD, like who gets it and why, and what it is like to have PTSD.

Chapter 1

BRIEF RELEVANT HISTORY OF PTSD

Symptoms of PTSD resulting from trauma are as old as humanity. References to such symptoms can be identified in the Old Testament of the Bible and in Greek mythology.

In more recent times, physicians during and after the Civil War described symptoms of PTSD, and suggested causes and remedies. World War I brought us the term *shell shock* to describe symptoms. Some physicians during that conflict learned that treating an afflicted soldier with a few days of rest with understanding caretakers and returning him to his combat unit (rather than evacuating him) resulted in far fewer long-term disabilities. After the war, interest in the problem waned.

Interest in the problem revived with the advent of World War II, which brought us the term *combat fatigue*. Experience from the previous war had to be relearned. A new and effective treatment was discovered. Combat veterans suffering a nervous reaction were given Amytal interviews as soon as possible after the traumatic incident and relived the incident and abreacted. The emotional discharge while reliving a traumatic event during abreaction relieved many symptoms and helped reduce long term symptoms. (*Amytal* is a barbiturate, and when given intravenously it can work like hypnosis in bringing out memories and emotions. *Abreaction* is the term describing vigorous emotional discharge associated with reliving a particular traumatic event).

After World War II, Veterans Administration physicians gave many combat veterans a diagnosis of *Anxiety Neurosis*. The cause of such symptoms was felt to be undiagnosed problems that existed prior to service. A "normal" individual was not expected to suffer lasting effects from the experience of combat, no matter how intense or prolonged. As a medical student starting in 1947, and then as a psychiatric resident in the fifties, I was taught this general concept of emotional problems suffered by war veterans. The concept stigmatized any problems related to war experience, since the existence of a problem indicated a character defect of some type.

5

During the fifties, we also began to see veterans of the Korean conflict who suffered from similar symptoms. Once again following the conflict in Vietnam, many veterans had persistent symptoms. They were unable to relate to a government agency like the Veterans Administration. Consequently, many of them started getting together to start *Rap Groups* to discuss their problems. After a time, some professionals became involved with the groups. These professionals gradually began to publish their experiences and findings. In the late seventies, the Veterans Administration started a *Vet Center* program for Vietnam veterans who did not feel comfortable coming to existing VA facilities. Rap groups were also conducted in these centers. Rap group experience therefore contributed to the development of a body of knowledge that finally led to the establishment of the diagnosis of PTSD that first appeared in *DSM-III* in 1980.

Professional resistance to the new diagnosis has always been a problem. Even in the Veterans Administration, most psychiatrists I dealt with after 1980 felt it was not a valid diagnosis and refused to consider this diagnosis for their patients. Although acceptance of PTSD on the part of professionals has gradually increased, there are still many who question the validity of the diagnosis, and therefore do not consider it when evaluating patients.

During the past several years, interest in the identification and treatment of PTSD has been increasing. More books and papers are being published. Hopefully, this trend will continue. There is now more being written about prevention and early intervention, which can greatly reduce the chronic disability associated with prolonged PTSD. Because this disorder results from a great variety of traumatic experiences in addition to war, it is very common in the general population. I hope that more professionals will be identifying and treating PTSD as time goes by.

Chapter 2

UNDERSTANDING PTSD:
VULNERABILITY, PREDISPOSITION, STIGMA

Knowledge and understanding of attitudes toward PTSD are critical if one is to deal with this important problem. Cultural learning determines many of our attitudes toward those suffering from symptoms of the disorder. A review of relevant attitudes, and factors influencing those attitudes, can therefore be helpful.

One important factor is the commonly held belief that a period of service in the military should be expected of everyone, especially young men. If this period of service includes participation in a war, it helps the young man grow up and develops character. Since participation in military combat is considered patriotic and glorious, the virtues of being a good soldier are extolled. A good example of this generally held view of war and manhood is sometimes referred to as the *John Wayne syndrome.* John Wayne starred in many movies that exemplified the attitudes that war proves the mettle of a man, is glorious, patriotic, and never causes undue fear, or other problems that a few stiff drinks won't straighten out. Wartime military experience is often considered a Rite of Passage for young men in our culture. Therefore, any residual emotional problems from these experiences tend to carry a stigma. The young man will therefore deny symptoms, and will not complain. In recent years it has been recognized that many women, such as nurses, also suffer the consequences of military combat even though they do not carry guns.

DSM-III-R indicates that in PTSD, "The person has experienced an event that is outside the range of usual human experience and that would be markedly distressing to almost anyone." This verifies that PTSD is a *normal* rather than a pathological reaction to trauma, since it is recognized that everyone has strong feelings and emotional reactions to traumatic experiences, and everyone has a breaking point. Therefore, it is possible for a normal person with no predisposition to suffer from PTSD, which is a complete reversal of traditional attitudes already reviewed. Unfortunately, it will take time for this relatively new under-standing of trauma to change the stigma associated with PTSD.

In my own experience, I felt terribly frightened on the first day of combat. Because of previous conditioning (John Wayne was never scared), I felt there was something wrong with me, that I was not as much of a man as my friends, that I was therefore inferior. I was unable to recognize that my emotions were perfectly normal under the circumstances, and I hid my shameful feelings from others (as they were also doing). Only later did I understand my other normal responses, such as numbing, denial, dissociative states, and feelings of omnipotence ("It can't happen to me"). I was confused and frightened when I observed friends who suddenly froze and were unable to move or even talk, another perfectly normal response to trauma.

As with other measures of human ability, the ability to tolerate stress is not the same for all. Using military combat as an example, everyone exposed to a given stress does not succumb with symptoms of PTSD at the same time. One individual will be first to succumb, another will be second, then a third, and finally, someone will be last. Understanding reasons for the sequence is important.

In describing factors relevant to this sequence, I find it helpful to use examples from physical illness. If someone with a common cold comes to work in an office employing ten people, perhaps two other people in the office will get a cold. If three people in that office keep working with colds, others may start getting colds. Those who get sick are not stigma-tized in any way and are apt to get sympathy. We assume that the individual who succumbed first may not have been getting proper rest or diet. The example also demonstrates that intensity and duration of exposure, as well as resistance, are important factors. Intensity of expo-sure is important. The employee sitting next to the one with the cold, getting sneezed on and coughed at is more likely to get sick. The factors of intensity, duration, and resistance appear to play a part in most or all instances of illness, whether physical or emotional. Recent research has demonstrated that the more severe the trauma, the more severe the symptoms of PTSD and the longer the period of necessary treatment. Response to treatment is faster when symptoms are less severe.

An additional factor playing a part in resistance and vulnerability to illness is what I have been calling the concept of *stacking*. Again, using the common cold as an example, if an individual has reduced resistance because of insufficient rest or poor diet, a sore throat may be the first symptom. That further lowers resistance, so exposure to the common cold is more likely to cause infection. The cold further lowers resistance, so one may more easily succumb to a strep throat or pneumonia, and so on. The sequence is both logical and simple. As more factors are stacked, resistance gets progressively lower.

The above example demonstrates that the more factors stacked, the greater the vulnerability. This general concept is helpful in understanding the development of PTSD without the stigma that is often attached to it. Generally we are more comfortable with this concept when it is applied to physical illness.

We are all aware that some days we feel so well that it takes a lot to get us angry or upset. Other days it may not take very much. If we are upset by personal problems, not sleeping well for some reason, have a headache or back pain, those are apt to be the days when it doesn't take much. When a woman is raped on that kind of day, her emotional response to the experience will be even stronger, and she is more likely to suffer long term effects of PTSD. The soldier who has been under fire for days, sleeping poorly if at all, maybe cold and hungry, will not deal with an intensely distressing traumatic event as well as when fresh and well rested. The soldier is therefore more at risk for developing PTSD, since the concept of stacking applies.

Vulnerability and predisposition to PTSD in response to trauma are therefore influenced by several factors. The first of these factors involves the concept of stacking. As already described, the vulnerability of the individual at the moment of trauma involves the number and severity of current stressors, lack of sleep, fatigue, physical illness, and so on. The more factors stacked, the greater the vulnerability.

Another factor influencing vulnerability is the similarity of the current trauma to a past trauma. This may be considered a type of predisposition. For example, we have literature regarding the higher incidence of emotional disturbances in soldiers who saw combat in *Operation Desert Storm* who had previously seen combat in Vietnam. I personally saw Vietnam combat veterans who became disabled by symptoms of PTSD when their reserve units were activated and they started combat training before being shipped to the Middle East. Their symptoms at that time were apparently more severe than they had been following combat in Vietnam. More recent research has found that the frequency of PTSD is much higher for soldiers who were physically abused during childhood.

Another example would be a woman who was sexually abused or raped at a young age. She may have gradually readjusted after the trauma, but if raped again even after many years, she would be more likely to suffer more powerful emotional reactions and more severe symptoms of PTSD than a woman who never had such a previous experience.

One factor seldom talked about is that the more *macho* an individual tends to be, the less acceptable are human frailties. Such a person finds it more difficult to accept the strong emotions in the face of trauma, especially fear. These people are therefore more vulnerable to PTSD following trauma. This can be a problem for women as well as for men.

There are a number of additional factors that influence the rate of PTSD when someone is exposed to trauma. As already indicated, both duration and intensity of trauma exert an important influence. The more intense the trauma, the more likely it will result in PTSD. For example, someone working in a factory when a large explosion occurs is more likely to suffer symptoms than a person working with machinery that occasionally malfunctions in a potentially injurious manner. However, if the latter worker experiences enough near misses and comes close to serious injury repeatedly over a period of time, succumbing with PTSD symptoms becomes more likely. Here we see both the factors of duration and stacking at work. The factor of duration usually involves the concept of stacking.

Physical injury is another factor that increases the likelihood of PTSD. In the example of duration above, if the worker were physically injured by one of the machine malfunctions, PTSD symptoms are more apt to develop. Likewise, if someone gets injured in an auto accident, the possibility of developing PTSD is greater. The soldier injured in combat is also more likely to suffer symptoms of PTSD than the soldier who did not sustain physical injury. The certain conviction that death is at hand appears to be an important factor in determining if one will suffer from PTSD. This factor appears to be more important than the severity of injury, since many individuals with relatively minor injuries develop severe symptoms. This has historically presented problems with the rating of disability for PTSD. For the Veterans Administration and for state workmans compensation boards, lack of serious physical injury has raised questions about the existence or seriousness of PTSD symptoms.

Helplessness is another factor that increases the likelihood of PTSD. For example, a woman who is assaulted but able to fight back is not as likely to have long term symptoms as the woman who is beaten and becomes helpless and unable to resist. The soldier who can return fire at the enemy is in better shape than the one who is pinned helplessly by artillery fire, and able only to seek shelter and cower in fear. The prisoner of war who is beaten and intimidated regularly without ability to resist is likewise a candidate for PTSD. Most former prisoners of war therefore suffer from symptoms of PTSD.

Age is another factor that can influence vulnerability to PTSD. Young children do not feel they are in good control of their surroundings or able to deal competently with adults. Trauma therefore tends to be more frightening for them and more likely to cause symptoms of PTSD. As children grow older and more mature, their self-confidence in handling the unexpected gradually improves. The likelihood and severity of PTSD in response to trauma therefore gradually diminishes with age. However, as people reach an advanced age, their self-confidence in dealing with emergencies and trauma starts to falter. The older they get, the possibility of PTSD resulting from trauma gradually increases. The very young and the very old are most vulnerable.

While working at a Veterans Administration Medical Center I diagnosed and treated hundreds of World War II veterans suffering from PTSD. Most of these veterans were ground combat soldiers. Only rarely were Air Force veterans seen except for those who became POW's. It is possible that combat airmen have a lower rate of PTSD, despite high losses and many injuries, because they flew home to respite. They had a period of rest in relative safety with more normal conditions before the next mission. Their duration of stress is limited and relatively short compared to soldiers who can be under fire for weeks or months on end, both day and night. This is another example of how duration of stress is an important factor.

Another factor that appears to influence the rate of PTSD is the individual's degree of emotional lability. Some people seem to keep an even disposition almost no matter what happens and have been that way their entire life. Others tend to have a rather strong emotional response to everything that happens. They are labile or volatile rather than even tempered. Most people are somewhere between these two extremes. There is literature, particularly with war-related trauma, that individuals who are strong emotional responders are more likely to suffer lasting symptoms of PTSD than those who are even tempered.

Genetic factors must be included on any list of factors that can influence the rate of PTSD. The role of such factors is unclear at this time.

After the above review of factors that influence the rate of PTSD, I would like to return briefly to the issue of stigma. Stigma is important because those with the problem usually won't talk about it, and will even deny symptoms when questioned. If we are to obtain the information and treat the patient successfully, our own attitudes must be free of stigma. There is a review of traditional attitudes in Chapter 1 that explains why symptoms are unacceptable to the patient, who tries to hide the shame. Therefore, the first complaint to a physician is likely to be a physical symptom rather than emotional distress.

The incidence of physical and medical problems is greatly increased in patients with PTSD. Recent literature confirms the increased rate of medical problems in patients suffering from disorders involving high anxiety and stress. These problems will be discussed further in other parts of this book.

The issue of PTSD resulting from trauma is best seen in overall perspective. When one is initially traumatized and overwhelmed, emotional reactions and symptoms tend to be severe. With time, however, symptoms usually diminish gradually. This may be seen with depression, where a person is initially overwhelmed by the death of a loved one. With time we can expect a gradual reduction of symptoms and distress. Everyone reacts to trauma with strong emotions, and the upsetting emotions usually subside gradually. With PTSD, therefore, the diagnosis is considered to be *Acute PTSD* during the first six months after trauma. When symptoms last more than six months, it is referred to as *Chronic or Prolonged PTSD*. In some cases, people who gradually recovered from acute symptoms suffer a return of acute symptoms at a later date. It can occur months or years later, unpredictably, and it can occur after many years. For example, many war veterans have reexperienced acute symptoms forty or fifty years after the original war trauma. This is referred to as *Delayed PTSD*.

SECTION II
DESCRIPTION OF SYMPTOMS

This section provides an in depth review of every symptom, each symptom comprising an individual chapter. The first seventeen symptoms (the ones in quotes) are taken directly from *DSM–III–R,* and the last nineteen symptoms are additional ones that I have come to recognize by personal experience in treating patients over the years.

Chapter 3

"RECURRENT AND INTRUSIVE DISTRESSING RECOLLECTIONS OF THE EVENT"

The word *recollections* in the heading above can be misleading, since recollections are memories. Of course it is always true that going back to a traumatic memory is distressing. However, for the patient with PTSD,[1] any return to the traumatic memory can start *ruminations,* which are an actual reliving of the experience, with the full emotional impact of the original experience. It is similar in these respects to a nightmare in which one relives a traumatic episode in living color, exactly as it happened, with the identical feelings and emotions, except that ruminations occur during the day. Ruminations are therefore far more disturbing and upsetting than memories, and more traumatic. I prefer to use the word ruminations rather than memories or recollections because it conveys a more accurate description of these terribly disturbing experiences that are the essence of PTSD. Memories and ruminations are therefore entirely different.

An important characteristic of ruminations is that they are not conscious. If you could ask an individual what he or she is thinking about, he or she would say, "Nothing." A person is aware only of the effects and aggravation of symptoms. When asked about spending time with traumatic memories, the patient is apt to deny doing so. One may not be aware of ruminations for hours at a time.

During ruminations, when the event is reexperienced with the full emotional impact of the original episode, the individual is traumatized emotionally to the same degree as with the original event, each and every time the event is reexperienced. It is always a most upsetting experience, whether the trauma occurred one year ago, ten years ago, or fifty years ago. "It is always like yesterday," is a common expression used to describe this most important symptom of PTSD, since it remains fresh and clear in every detail, and just as painful and upsetting. The emotional impact of ruminations does not diminish with time, as we usually

15

expect to occur with most painful life experiences. This distinct and central feature of PTSD[2] changes the treatment considerations that apply to most other diagnostic categories.

To make matters worse, the traumatic event is usually reexperienced and relived many times each day. Those who suffer from PTSD can therefore spend many hours every day repeatedly reliving the event. The intensity of emotional distress escalates as the total time spent with these ruminations increases. The cumulative number of hours per day spent with ruminations therefore determines the level of intensity of overall emotional distress and suffering and the intensity of symptoms. For this reason I consider PTSD to be one of the most intensely distressing and disabling emotional afflictions from which a human being can suffer.

Another quality of ruminations often not appreciated is the speed with which they can begin. The rumination, or reliving of a traumatic event, frequently starts the instant a trigger[3] is encountered. It is like the snapping on of an electric switch. The instant a trigger is seen or heard, the patient starts ruminating. For example, a patient can suddenly see something move, and a rumination begins in less than one second.

For some individuals, such as abused children or war veterans, there were multiple traumatic events rather than only one.[4] In that instance, there may be more than one traumatic experience that the person spends time with. Therefore, this individual can drift into ruminating about one of two or three distinct events. These tend to be the most traumatic and most upsetting of all the events. I have never seen a patient suffering from PTSD from multiple traumatic events who spends time ruminating with a great number of different events. It is always one, or just a few of the most traumatic events that are repeatedly reexperienced. War veterans often ask, "Why can't I go back to some of the good memories, why is it always the worst one?" I can only answer, "That's the way it works." That appears to be true because it is not possible to return to good memories of war without the associated traumatic ruminations also returning. This feature holds true for PTSD from any cause, since related memories trigger the reliving of traumatic experiences.

My personal experience with ruminations[5] occurred at a time there was no understanding of the problem, and talking to anyone about it was out of the question. The conviction that I was the only one so afflicted increased my shame and feelings of stigma. For hours at a time I was unable to control ruminations and distress. The lack of control and feeling helpless and overwhelmed was frightening, I lived in fear of it happening again, and often feared I was going crazy. Night was the worst time. Lying in bed seemed to bring on the problem, and I dreaded the night and going to bed. Those were terrible times for me, and the memory is still clear. This experience sensitized me to the importance of learning control to end the awful helplessness. I therefore always give patients tools with which to fight so they are no longer helpless in the face of symptoms. They then have the power, rather than the symptoms having the power. This alone provides a great deal of relief. Most patients suffering from PTSD have had experiences similar to mine, and also were never able to talk about it.

Many triggers are known to set off the process of reliving a traumatic experience. After a time people start to recognize some of the things that trigger their discomfort, and try to avoid them. For example, someone who was physically abused as a child[6] may start painful ruminations while watching a movie or TV show in which a child is punished or injured. For a person who suffers PTSD from an auto accident, memories and ruminations can be started by seeing an accident on the highway, by seeing a particular model or color car, by passing a specific type of intersection, or by a multitude of other specific triggers. For a war veteran, seeing a picture of a military vehicle, hearing a war report, passing a military convoy on the highway, or seeing or hearing a helicopter could be triggers. Since the mind works so quickly, one thing relating to another can become a trigger. For example, someone could enter the clothing department of a department store. The thought of clothing could jump to a thought of belts, which could quickly jump to the memory of beatings with a belt they experienced as a child, and then to ruminations. For a war veteran, it could start with the sight of a ship. The next thought could jump to the ship that brought them to a war zone, the next thought going to combat, and finally to the particular traumatic event that causes the most intense emotional response. The entire process takes only a fraction of a second. A trigger can therefore be anything that even remotely resembles an aspect of the traumatic event, or an anniversary of the event. Since there are so many triggers that can start the ruminations, it is not possible to prevent or avoid every one of them. However, one can work on keeping them to a minimum.

Another type of trigger often difficult to catch results from hypervigilance related to the conditions of the trauma. For example, someone who did intelligence and undercover work developed a high state of alertness that was necessary twenty-four hours a day in order to stay alive. They checked out everyone they saw for dress, manner, behavior, the way they talk and move, bulges indicating concealed weapons, and many other details for indications of potential danger. This "way of life" that was developed for self-preservation is difficult to stop, even though it is no longer needed. However, the watchfulness in itself becomes a trigger for traumatic experiences, since it leads to various memories and ruminations. In like manner, a combat veteran can drive along a country road and find himself looking for terrain features that offer hiding places, or are potential tank maneuver areas. I refer to this as *playing war games.* Such behavior is another trigger that must be stopped if one is to reduce ruminations and consequent symptoms of PTSD. Although these are only two examples, this type of hypervigilance can occur with PTSD caused by any type of trauma.

Subliminal perceptions can also serve as triggers. Ruminations can therefore be started by sights and sounds that do not enter conscious awareness. The momentary glimpse of an individual resembling the one associated with the trauma, the glimpse of a particular place related to the trauma, or a faint sound, are examples. The war veteran who lives near a military post may spend time with ruminations triggered by the faint sounds of distant gunfire not consciously heard.

Learning to avoid triggers therefore becomes an important part of reducing symptoms. For example, the combat veteran[7] learns to turn the TV channel quickly if reports of war or violence begin. The veteran also learns to avoid places that are triggers. Driving near military installations or going to watch military parades are examples. For the individual injured in an auto accident, avoiding particular areas or intersections may be helpful. When a trigger is encountered, one must learn to keep the impact to a minimum by limiting the time spent with the resulting rumination.

Since there is amnesia for a variable portion of the traumatic event, there is no conscious memory of many things that could be triggers. A patient can therefore go to a particular place or see a specific object or type of person, and not know what caused the emotional reaction.

In my own experience, it took time for me to recognize that specific triggers started the problems. War movies were the first of many culprits I became aware of, and I recall strictly avoiding them. I also tried to stay away from places with posters advertising war movies, since seeing a poster could start the process. Passing a funeral also started memories of death and consequent ruminations, and it was many years before I was able to attend a funeral. It took me much longer to recognize other triggers, such as talking to fellow combat veterans about the war, news reports of military matters, and letters from other survivors of my unit.

Those suffering from PTSD, whatever the cause, usually work very hard at avoiding triggers that bring on such painful ruminations. It is therefore one of the important reasons why symptoms are not mentioned or admitted, and part of why most women who are raped never tell anyone about it. Simply mentioning anything related to the trauma could trigger ruminations and their disturbing consequences. It is simply too upsetting.

Stress from any source is another important trigger for traumatic memories and consequent ruminations. The stress could be a marital problem, a financial problem, car trouble, or a problem on the job. Health problems and physical pain are common stressors that also become triggers. I have heard patients say, "When the pain starts, it opens the door to the bad memories." I therefore teach patients that whenever they experience stress, they must work harder to avoid spending time with ruminations. Knowing that stress will trigger the traumatic ruminations, the individual can be prepared for them when the stress occurs. This knowledge can prevent being caught off guard, with symptoms becoming painful before one is aware of what is going on.

Those with chronic pain conditions have special problems, since the stress caused by pain keeps triggering ruminations. The need to keep concentration elsewhere requires almost constant effort, and pain programs are often helpful.

My own experience includes a femur fracture a few years ago near the site of war-related bone damage. I required surgical procedures and became toxic from infection. The intense and prolonged pain and general physical distress triggered combat nightmares I had not experienced for many years. This indicated that I also had ruminations I was not aware of. It is an example of how stress caused by severe pain triggers the problem. My war-related memories and consequent ruminations were also apparently triggered by the fracture and orthopedic care in a hospital.

Spending time with traumatic ruminations is in itself a stress that triggers more time with ruminations. Without special effort to avoid it, some individuals can slip into episodes of continuous ruminations lasting hours, even days. I have known individuals who remained in one position, without moving, for two or more days at a time.

For most people, sitting around with nothing special in mind can start thoughts drifting to worries and unpleasant memories. When one who suffers from PTSD is bored, the traumatic rumination is usually *invited*. A routine activity that does not require concentration can also allow the mind to wander and therefore lead to the painful rumination. A helpful concept is that of a vacuum. I tell patients that when the mind is not actively occupied, it leaves a void or vacuum that is quickly filled by a painful rumination. We can concentrate fully on only one thing at a time. Consequently, learning to keep one's mind actively occupied is essential to reducing time with ruminations and consequent distressing PTSD symptoms.

Another important characteristic of ruminations already described is that the patient is usually not consciously aware of spending time with them. Because of this lack of conscious awareness, the individual will often deny that such a problem exists. One becomes aware only of the results of spending time with ruminations. Results include escalating discomforts such as anxiety[8] and depression, irritability with temper outbursts, and a host of other symptoms that may or may not be on the *DSM-III-R* list of symptoms. For example, if the individual tries to read, the same sentence must be reread time and again because it is not registering. That should immediately tell someone their concentration is elsewhere, most likely on a rumination. Those suffering from PTSD usually can't concentrate on reading at least part of the time. I knew one war veteran who claimed he forgot how to read, since he had this problem most of the time. In treatment, the patient learns to recognize when ruminations are starting, and to do something quickly to keep bad time with ruminations to a minimum. This will be reviewed in more detail in a later section.

Some individuals spend more time than average with ruminations. They may spend many hours most days reliving traumatic events. While ruminating they are elsewhere, and not with their family, simply unaware of what goes on around them. Sometimes a day or two, even more, can elapse before individuals respond to their surroundings in an appropriate manner. I have already mentioned patients who lie or sit in one place, without moving, for up to two days at a time. There is usually complete amnesia for these long periods of time spent with ruminations. This is one type of dissociative period seen with PTSD, and dissociative periods will be covered as a separate symptom.

Since someone reliving traumatic events for long periods like this is not sleeping, sleep deprivation symptoms may complicate the problem. I have never been able to separate sleep deprivation symptoms from the various other symptoms associated with PTSD since both may cause similar symptoms. Medical problems can be another complication of the extended periods described. For example, if someone goes two days without eating, drinking, or taking needed medication, conditions like diabetes, heart problems and epilepsy could be adversely affected.

An additional problem with ruminations is comparable to partially awakening with a nightmare, and continuing the nightmare while up and around, possibly interacting with others. A similar thing can occur with daytime ruminations. The patient is accused by family members of saying things or threatening others. The patient may accuse them of lying, therefore, because there is no conscious recollection of these episodes. In some instances, this can become a serious problem.

It is important to remember that children and adolescents[9] can suffer from PTSD, as well as adults. The child who is preoccupied and not paying attention in school could be experiencing ruminations of traumatic events. The young adolescent who starts drinking and changing behavior may also suffer from PTSD, and should be questioned about ruminations and other symptoms. Many adults have PTSD caused by childhood trauma, usually physical or sexual abuse. They may continue to suffer from symptoms until they receive appropriate treatment.

Over the years, I have developed the conviction that ruminations, or time reliving traumatic events, is the key to the diagnosis and treatment of PTSD. The patient is aware of distress, upsets, and various life problems, but is usually not aware of spending time with traumatic ruminations that cause the problems. As already described, the more total time one spends with ruminations each day, the higher the level of emotional distress, and the greater the number and severity of symptoms. Therefore, the level and intensity of distress, and the number and severity of specific symptoms, are directly proportional to the total length of time spent with traumatic ruminations. I tell patients, "The more time you spend with ruminations each day, the more the symptoms on the PTSD list will give you trouble." The example of a steam boiler is often helpful. The longer the boiler is fired, the higher the pressure and the more powerful the explosion when it finally blows. I also tell them that spending time with traumatic ruminations gives energy and power to their symptoms. To emphasize the importance of this issue, I often say, "If you could stop spending time with ruminations, you would not have a problem." Patients therefore come to understand quickly that working on reducing daily time with ruminations reduces the severity of all their other problems and symptoms, and is the key to feeling better. During treatment, no matter what the issue or symptom, time with ruminations is a key factor. In the treatment section, we will review ways in which this knowledge is used to control symptoms.

Chapter 4

"RECURRING DISTRESSING DREAMS
OF THE EVENT"

Distressing dreams, or nightmares of the traumatic event, have some special qualities in PTSD. For a period of time after the original event, the individual reexperiences, or relives the experience during the dream exactly as it happened, with the same full emotional impact. Nightmares of this type can persist for many years. I know many World War II veterans who continue to suffer such nightmares after fifty years.[10] These veterans may not recognize what they see in some of the bad dreams, which is consistent with the amnesia that is usually associated with PTSD. I can personally recall nightmares of events while I was carried in a stretcher. Those events occurred during the five days for which I have complete amnesia, and they were probably replays of exactly what happened.

After a period of months or years, some or all of the nightmares can change in nature. They may become frightening dreams of another type, such as being chased, falling, smothering, drowning, or being harmed in various other ways, rather than a reliving of the actual experience. The patient may have no further nightmares in which the traumatic event is reexperienced in total or even in part. Frightening dreams of any type can therefore be associated with PTSD. They need not be a reliving of the event to be considered nightmares associated with the diagnosis. Many patients report that after a nightmare, they feel more upset and tense the entire next day.

Some individuals become aware that they try to change the nightmare to a more pleasant ending, or to a happy ending. The next day they can recall their attempts to make such changes during the nightmare, but the efforts are usually unsuccessful. I have met only a few people who succeeded in this endeavor. They developed the ability to quickly change the dream to a pleasant one with a happy ending. When capable of doing this consistently, they no longer have a disturbing nightmare problem, although the dream and effort to change it are often remembered as an unpleasant experience.

Since we tend to dream about the things that have been on our mind during the day, frequency of nightmares with PTSD[11] is strongly influenced by the amount of time spent with daytime ruminations. I therefore advise patients that they can reduce the nightmare problem by learning to reduce the *bad* time spent with ruminations during the day. This effort provides the individual with power to deal with nightmares, since something done actively during waking hours has a positive effect.

Some individuals admit to nightmares, but completely deny daytime ruminations. I explain to them that we usually dream about things that have been on our mind during the day. However, since the ruminations are not usually conscious, we may not be aware of spending time with them. For most, this may initially be difficult to believe, and it is often vigorously denied.

Some PTSD patients can experience nightmares many times each night. Others report that the problem is infrequent. However, many people remember few or none of their dreams and nightmares, and often deny the problem completely. If questioned, a spouse may report one or more episodes each night in which the patient moans, shouts or moves violently, indicating nightmares the patient does not remember. Some wives say they leave the bed on nights when the thrashing continues so they can get some sleep. Many individuals describe themselves as restless sleepers, saying they are "all over the bed," with sheets and blankets tangled when they get up in the morning. Some can awaken on the floor, or are awakened during the night when they fall out of bed, but do not remember a nightmare. Other indications of nightmares can be awakening in a different location, or having something in bed that wasn't there upon retiring. This is another unique feature of nightmares associated with PTSD that can help make the diagnosis.

When awakening from a nightmare, the patient with PTSD often has difficulty awakening fully. There can be an extended period during which the patient is half awake and half asleep. During this period the patient may get up or do various things that are a continuation of the nightmare. For example, a war veteran can start beating or strangling his wife next to him in bed since he is fighting with an enemy soldier. He doesn't stop until he is fully awakened, when the half and half period has ended. Many veterans have slept in a separate bedroom for years because of great concern that they could harm their wives. Another individual could get out of bed and start smashing things in the house before awakening fully. Here again he was continuing a fight with the enemy. In some instances, individuals awaken in the morning with something frightening in their bed, like a gun or knife. This indicates that the person was up and did something while not fully awake, and then went back to deep sleep. They do not remember the nightmare, or getting out of bed. Awakening with a gun or knife in bed appears to be in some way related to a nightmare, even if it is only partially related to reliving the traumatic experience. Patients can awaken in another room of their house, or while walking on the street fully dressed, and not remember leaving the bed. Such experiences are always frightening, and I feel they are diagnostic for PTSD. Becoming fully awake as quickly as possible after a nightmare is therefore important. If not fully awake the individual can return to bed and to deep sleep, and continue the same nightmare.

While awakening from a nightmare, individuals are often disoriented for a period of time, not sure of where they are until fully awake. This is why most patients are helped by keeping a light on during the night. If able to see familiar objects in their bedroom, full awakening and orientation can take place faster.

The described behaviors associated with a nightmare and not remembered are usually considered to be dissociative episodes. The confusion and disorientation on awakening is likewise considered dissociative in nature.

On awakening from a nightmare, the individual may be trembling with fear, with heavy breathing and pounding heart. Sweating is common. Some individuals are wet with sweat, and before returning to bed must shower, change their pajamas and even the bed sheets. Profuse sweating on awakening from a nightmare is another symptom that is fairly unique to PTSD, and specific questions are necessary to elicit the information.

After a nightmare, the patient gets out of bed when sufficiently awake and does some typical things. Pacing around the house for a period of time is common. While walking around, the patient may look out of windows for signs of danger, and check to be sure that doors and windows are locked. (Specific questions must be asked in order to elicit such behavior.) Then comes a period during which the person tries to settle down, relax, and get concentration away from the nightmare and onto something different and calming. Many will sit and watch TV or a videotape as a means of changing focus and relaxing. Others prefer to listen to soft music or read. When the individual feels sufficiently relaxed, sleep may again be possible.

The period of time it takes to get back to sleep after a nightmare can vary. Some individuals remain awake for the remainder of the night after every nightmare. Others are able to get back to sleep after a variable period of relaxation, staying awake for the remainder of the night only occasionally. One aim of treatment is to improve sleep by helping people learn to relax more rapidly and effectively after a nightmare, so sleep is again possible.

Chapter 5

"SUDDEN ACTING OR FEELING AS IF THE TRAUMATIC EVENT WERE RECURRING (INCLUDES A SENSE OF RELIVING THE EXPERIENCE, ILLUSIONS, HALLUCINATIONS, AND DISSOCIATIVE 'FLASHBACK' EPISODES, EVEN THOSE THAT OCCUR UPON AWAKENING OR WHEN INTOXICATED)."

During the day, an individual who is peacefully walking along the street can suddenly and abruptly go berserk, start running or shouting, and may assault other people in the area. This can happen in a "flashback" episode during which the person is suddenly reliving the original traumatic experience. This reliving of the trauma is comparable to the PTSD nightmare, except that it does not start during sleep. The individual behaves as he did during the original traumatic episode, including similar physical action. A combat veteran[12] reliving an incident may see enemy soldiers who must be attacked rather than ordinary people on the street. Since he behaves as he did during the original incident, he may injure others. When the episode is over and the person awakens, there is no memory of the incident.

Episodes like this are triggered by something seen, heard, or experienced through any of the senses. The trigger could be the sound of an airplane, the sight of a military vehicle, a specific odor, or passing a person who looks like the assailant.

These episodes are described in the literature[13] but are apparently rare. I have never personally met a person with PTSD who had this type of violent experience. However, I know a Vietnam Veteran who had related experiences. He has a fenced-in backyard. For a period of months, every time he looked over the back fence to the next house, he would see a river, not a shallow gully, and would see typical Vietnamese people across the river. He never acted on what he saw, and when he turned around he would return to his own house without incident. In this instance, the veteran did not reexperience one of the traumatic events related to his PTSD, the emotions were therefore not as strong, and he remembered what happened.

One of my personal friends is a Korean War Veteran. He has never had serious problems related to his war experiences. His most traumatic life threatening experience involved a North Korean Officer. One day during 1992 he was walking on the street with his wife when he suddenly left her and approached a Korean man.[14] When he walked back to his understanding wife she said, "You thought it was that North Korean Officer." He agreed. She asked, "What were you going to do?" He answered, "I guess I was going to kill him." The event was upsetting to my friend and illustrates another facet of this problem. Nothing like this ever happened to him before, and the original event occurred forty years ago.

The term *flashback* has become non-specific. People have been using the term to describe a daytime rumination or other experiences involving traumatic memories. When someone uses the term, therefore, a full description of the experience is necessary to ascertain exactly what the person means.

A related experience that could qualify as "sudden acting or feeling as if the traumatic event were recurring" is the period during a nightmare when the patient is partially awake, gets out of bed, and continues the behavior associated with the traumatic event. This was described more fully under the section on nightmares. However, such episodes are associated with sleep, rather than occurring during the day.

The described episodes are considered dissociative in nature. I have described illusions associated with such experiences, but I am not sure about hallucinations. During a flashback experience, I presume it is possible to see or hear things that are not actually there. When that is the case, it would be called a *hallucination*.

Chapter 6

"INTENSE PSYCHOLOGICAL DISTRESS AT EXPOSURE TO EVENTS THAT SYMBOLIZE OR RESEMBLE AN ASPECT OF THE TRAUMATIC EVENT, INCLUDING ANNIVERSARIES OF THE TRAUMA"

This symptom is closely related to the symptom of daytime ruminations already described. Exposure to events that symbolize or resemble an aspect of the traumatic event in some way trigger the problem. As previously described, one thought can lead to another in a fraction of a second, usually to the most painful memory. It is therefore possible for a great variety of stimuli to become triggers. For example, an individual with PTSD resulting from an auto accident while driving on an icy highway may find that the sight of snow and ice is a trigger, even when seen on television. A veteran of jungle warfare, such as in Vietnam, can have traumatic memories triggered by wet, rainy weather. An individual then starts ruminating, or reliving the traumatic event, resulting in a strong emotional reaction and worsening of various PTSD symptoms. This intense psychological distress is usually suffered without conscious awareness of the painful experience that is being relived since one is not conscious of ruminations. The individual is also frequently not consciously aware of the trigger. As already described, the more time spent with these ruminations, the stronger the emotional response, the higher the degree of distress, and the more symptoms of PTSD become evident. Patients therefore learn to avoid triggers if at all possible.

Anniversary reactions likewise involve triggers and the spending of more time with traumatic memories and ruminations. On the anniversary of a PTSD related trauma, memories and ruminations of the event are often triggered. Patients report that they become upset during a particular week or month of the year, and upon reflection realize it was the time of the offending trauma. In most instances, they were spending time with the distressing memory well before they became aware of the trigger. Some describe the problem in relation to a specific holiday, or in relation to an entire season of the year. For example, victims of rape or auto accidents may notice the anniversary reaction on the date of the incident each year. For a combat veteran, it could be the date he was shot down, the day he was severely injured, or the day he became a POW. Sometimes the anniversary can be non-specific. For example, a combat veteran can have increased PTSD symptoms and distress during a holiday, particularly Christmas. The memory of that holiday in a war zone can quickly lead to the most traumatic memories of war, resulting in ruminations.

Chapter 7

"EFFORTS TO AVOID THOUGHTS OR FEELINGS ASSOCIATED WITH THE TRAUMA"

As already discussed, a great variety of stimuli can trigger the traumatic memories. After a time, those suffering from PTSD learn to avoid specific triggers that cause ruminations and consequent severe symptoms of distress. Therefore, spending time with feelings, thoughts, or memories that are associated with the offending trauma are avoided. People often come to avoid particular thoughts and memories without recognizing the reason for doing so.

One example is an individual who suffers from PTSD related to a highway accident. This person may find that reminiscing about a pleasant auto travel vacation could trigger the traumatic memory, since both the enjoyable vacation and the accident involved automobiles on the road. Thinking about the city in which the accident occurred could likewise trigger the onset of painful memories. In this instance, the person would try to avoid thinking of anything related that could trigger their problem.

As previously explained, the mind works quickly. One thought leads to another in a fraction of a second, a process difficult to control. Therefore, one can try to avoid drifting into thoughts or memories that may lead a train of thought to upsetting places. An example has already been mentioned of war veterans who cannot think of pleasant events during wartime without also remembering the most distressing war memories.

Many other examples of this problem could be listed. A woman suffering PTSD from rape may think of having sex with her husband, and find that it leads to memories of the rape. Someone with PTSD resulting from being injured in a fire may avoid thoughts of their home furnace and heating system. These are examples of the thought process involved, and some ways in which people try to avoid spending time with traumatic memories.

As already described, the triggering of a traumatic memory or rumination requires prompt response, since reducing time with such a memory reduces distress and pain. Quickly diverting attention and concentration elsewhere appears to be the most effective way to achieve this goal.

Chapter 8

"EFFORTS TO AVOID ACTIVITIES OR SITUATIONS THAT AROUSE RECOLLECTIONS OF THE TRAUMA"

Avoiding activities or situations that trigger traumatic memories and ruminations is always a symptom of PTSD, since spending time in this manner is so painful and upsetting. Avoidance involves all the senses, since what is seen, heard, felt, smelled, or tasted can trigger the problem.

A Vietnam veteran with PTSD, for example, may avoid military areas or sounds, military or war movies, violence of any type on television, war or military news reports, crowded or noisy places, rivers or lakes, or the smell of meat being cooked or barbecued. The rape victim may avoid going out after dark, avoid lonely or crowded places, being close to a man, or even leaving the house alone. Someone injured in a traffic accident may avoid heavy traffic, certain areas or intersections, or may even refuse to enter a car. There can be various degrees of restriction of activity, movement, and travel for this reason. Some individuals are so fearful of encountering triggers they refuse to leave the safety of their home. Most people develop such avoidance behavior prior to treatment, and before they understand the reasons for their behavior.

There is a perverse aspect to this problem. Those suffering from PTSD are usually interested in and drawn to the very things that cause problems. For example, the war veteran is fascinated by a war movie or a military or war report, guns and weapons, a military parade or exhibition, or information about their region of combat. Such an individual will suffer from more time with ruminations after viewing something like this, but next time will do the very same thing. The reason for doing so is often rationalized by thoughts such as, "Maybe it could help my problem." I have known veterans who watch war movies or combat tapes regularly, are fascinated by them, and won't accept advice to stop. They refuse to believe that it aggravates their condition. They often say they enjoy them and feel it is helpful for them.

Those with PTSD from other causes may have similar perverse behavior. The individual who was traumatized by a chemical spill may be fascinated by movies about chemical spills or similar natural disasters. They may read books on the subject, or visit areas of recent disasters. They may visit places where hazardous chemicals are stored. Here again, there is often a lack of awareness of the distress and pain brought on by such activities. The appropriate connections are not made.

In like fashion, the individual who suffered abuse as a child can be fascinated by movies of child abuse, and the victim of an auto accident insists on watching a movie about auto accidents. They must also learn to stop doing the things that increase time with memories, ruminations, and the consequent suffering with PTSD symptoms.

Chapter 9

"INABILITY TO RECALL AN IMPORTANT ASPECT OF THE TRAUMA (PSYCHOGENIC AMNESIA)"

The individual suffering from PTSD usually has some degree of amnesia associated with the traumatic experience.[15] The degree of amnesia is variable. It can include one or more occurrences during the period of trauma, large portions of the period, or the entire period. There may be anterograde or retrograde amnesia,[16] so that periods of time before or after the trauma are not remembered. In my own case, I don't remember getting injured, but learned later that I remained conscious. I "woke up" in an army hospital five days later, without memory of those five days, but also without memory of a day or two before the injury. (I can't be sure of the number of days.) None of those memories have returned, fortunately. During the first few years I wanted to remember everything, but it is probably better that I didn't. I saw things in nightmares for a time from the period of amnesia, but the nightmares fortunately stopped.

Combat veterans often think they remember everything from the period of combat.[17] However, most of them suffering from PTSD report that after talking to friends, they were surprised to hear about battles or events they did not remember. Other veterans recognize that they have blank periods of variable duration. I have known combat veterans who have no memory of a year or more of combat. During nightmares they may see a particular episode, but on awakening there is still no recollection of the event.

Women with PTSD resulting from rape often don't remember a large part of the rape episode. It is not unusual for rape victims to remember nothing of the incident when they wake up at home, or at some time after the episode.

Women who were abused physically by a father in drunken rages usually recall at least some of the beatings. However, they often completely

deny any incidents of sexual abuse.[18] In some instances, they remember
going to bed with him to pacify him at such times, but deny that
anything sexual ever occurred. Alcoholic fathers who abuse their daugh-
ters physically often abuse them sexually as well. Therefore, when a
patient remembers only physical abuse, I assume there is a possibility
that sexual abuse also occurred.

In like manner, PTSD from any cause usually involves some degree of
amnesia. The portion of the episode not remembered is apt to be the
most traumatic part. Therefore, when the patient slips into rumination,
or reliving a trauma, it is most apt to be one of the most disturbing and
upsetting episodes, which are likely to be the ones not consciously
remembered. A fairly common and familiar example is related to auto
accidents. Partial amnesia can cause one driver to have a somewhat
different story than the other.

Chapter 10

"MARKEDLY DIMINISHED INTEREST IN SIGNIFICANT ACTIVITIES"

Family members often describe the individual suffering from PTSD as "a completely different person." One of the reasons they say this is that interests and activities have markedly changed. For example, the person may have been an enthusiastic golfer, home auto mechanic, gardener, or gourmet cook. After a trauma causing PTSD, the individual can have greatly reduced enthusiasm, or may have completely lost interest in one or many activities. In most instances, new interests have not emerged. This can leave someone time to spend without interest or activity. As previously described, boredom increases the time spent with traumatic memories and ruminations, aggravating all other symptoms.

This symptom appears to have several possible causes. Diminished interest could be caused by increased preoccupation with ruminations that consumes more time, energy, and focus of thought. It could be caused by inability to concentrate on the activity usually because ruminations are intrusive and make concentration difficult or impossible. There could be a feeling of being overwhelmed by symptoms, so one simply gives up on many activities. This may be accompanied by resignation, like, "I'm doomed," or, "I can't fight it anymore." Another possibility is that trauma can leave people feeling that they are different, not as good as others, no longer the same person, so that former activities are no longer felt to be appropriate, or confidence in ability is reduced or lost.

In the process of obtaining information, prior interests and activities must always be questioned. The person could have had hobbies, sports, and recreational activities in the past. A change in interest and enthusiasm about one's work or leisure time activities can often be a symptom of PTSD.

Chapter 11

"FEELING OF DETACHMENT OR ESTRANGEMENT FROM OTHERS"

After the trauma, an individual with PTSD is often described by family and friends as a changed person. One of the changes they notice is a degree of mistrust of others. This results in keeping a distance, even from those the individual was formerly very close to, including spouse and children. Getting close to another person, physically or emotionally, appears to cause intense discomfort for the patient. Many individuals feel comfortable only when completely alone. This results in frequent marital and family problems, and divorce is common. Many patients report that they avoid stores, crowds, or any situation where others can get physically close. For this reason, some will walk many flights of stairs rather than get into an elevator. Others are unable to work in a job that involves physical proximity to others, and may request transfer to another department, or leave the job entirely.

The patient tends to feel different from others, that communication with them is difficult or impossible, that someone who has not been through it simply could not possibly understand. Therefore, attempting to explain to anyone would be futile. The feeling of difference is also associated with stigma, as previously discussed. It leads to feelings of isolation, the conviction that others dislike or disapprove, all of which adds up to additional stress.

As with all other symptoms of PTSD, the degree of the problem is variable. There are some patients who are able to maintain fairly close relationships, while many others have serious marital and social problems. Some attempt to live their lives in complete isolation from the world, living far from others out in the country, or camping alone in the deep woods for long periods of time. Some talk about becoming a hermit deep in the woods where they won't see another person.

These problems may represent an attempt to avoid getting hurt or traumatized again. For example, combat veterans admit in group therapy that during the war, it was most upsetting when a close friend was injured or killed. They therefore recall avoiding new friendships with replacement troops, so it would not hurt so much when they were killed. They worked very hard at keeping distance from others, and developed a feeling of numbness toward distressing events (no feelings; "This isn't really happening"). Combat veterans therefore often recall developing the feeling of detachment and estrangement even before suffering the specific trauma that caused their PTSD.

The protective detachment appears to be associated with PTSD from all causes, and is seen to some degree in almost all PTSD patients. This detachment may be considered to be a dissociative symptom.

Chapter 12

"RESTRICTED RANGE OF AFFECT, E.G., UNABLE TO HAVE LOVING FEELINGS"

A great deal of this symptom has been discussed in the previous chapter. The PTSD patient is not usually comfortable with feelings and emotions, and getting emotionally or physically close to anyone would provoke anxiety and distress. The individual is therefore often torn between the conflicting love feelings for spouse and children and the inability to get close and show affection. Many patients respond to this conflict by avoiding family members, preferring to be alone.

A marriage is always strongly effected by PTSD in one spouse. The patient may say that love feelings are gone, or that they can't be expressed. Sexual impotence and loss of interest in lovemaking and sex are common. Sexual response can be reduced or completely gone. A spouse feels rejected and unloved, since expression and demonstration of love feelings are sharply reduced or entirely absent. Marital discord and divorce are common, and this symptom is usually involved in the marital problems.

Since the PTSD patient is uncomfortable with feelings or emotions of any type, all social contacts are effected. At work the individual may be viewed as antisocial, rigid, uninterested, and uncaring. Friendships suffer when the person appears distant and unconcerned. When friends are lost, the tendency toward social isolation is reinforced.

Since the PTSD patient desperately wants the social relationships that can't be handled, treatment includes specific suggestions for the problem.

Chapter 13

"SENSE OF A FORESHORTENED FUTURE, E.G., DOES NOT EXPECT TO HAVE A CAREER, MARRIAGE, OR CHILDREN, OR A LONG LIFE"

Patients suffering from PTSD often have this sense of a foreshortened future, although the strength of the feeling is variable. As indicated, they don't expect to live long, and therefore feel no need to make long range plans for their life. Intermediate and long term goals are pointless and no effort is made. It includes the feeling that their life is about over, that they have had it.

Plans for a career or promotion are consequently felt to be irrelevant or unnecessary, and efforts in this direction are apt to be half-hearted at best. If the individual is working, there are usually problems in getting along with others and tolerating supervision. Job promotions and work career are rarely considered, since day-to-day problems cause so much stress.

Similar attitudes apply to social areas of living. The individual does not foresee a good possibility for marriage, children, or family life, particularly since life is not expected to last long. Problems in feeling comfortable with those of the opposite sex contribute to such attitudes. Social comfort with those of the same sex is also usually low, adding to the feeling of isolation.

The sense of a foreshortened future is not usually verbalized. Specific questions can elicit the information at times. In some instances, family members can supply the information, since they may recall the patient expressing such sentiments in the past.

We can only speculate on the reasons for this symptom. Perhaps the traumatized individual feels at some level like the life threatening trauma has actually taken the best part of life, so that a normal life span is no longer possible. Perhaps the symptoms of PTSD are so overwhelming that the person feels unable to carry on much longer. PTSD patients

41

often talk of their abilities (prior to trauma) in past tense, like the good things are all gone. These feelings could also contribute to the problem.

Chapter 14

"DIFFICULTY FALLING OR STAYING ASLEEP"

Most people have trouble falling asleep when they go to bed tense and worried. Unable to relax, they lie in bed reviewing problems and concerns. Lying in the dark without purposeful activity to occupy the mind appears to aggravate the problem. PTSD patients[19] usually have such sleep problems because ruminations and upsets during the day result in tension and worry at bedtime.

The PTSD patient must be asked specific questions about how long it takes to fall asleep since this is an important piece of information. An individual may say it takes about one hour to get to sleep. When asked if it takes longer some nights, the patient may reveal that it can take 2 or 3 hours to get to sleep, and some nights even longer.

After questions about how long it takes to get to sleep, the patient must be asked about the average number of awakenings each night. Most people who are under stress report more awakenings during the night. Many PTSD patients report a variable number of awakenings, some nights two or three, other nights six or more. Sleeping through the night is uncommon for these patients.[20]

It is also important to ask the patient how long it takes to get back to sleep after awakening during the night. Here again, the time can be quite variable. Most PTSD patients take at least one half to one hour to get back to sleep during the night. Sometimes it takes much longer, or the patient can be awake for the remainder of the night even without a nightmare. Those who awaken on the average of several times each night and remain awake for long periods get little sleep. They may therefore have difficulty staying awake during the day, and PTSD symptoms may be complicated by symptoms of sleep deprivation.

If one is awakened during the night by a nightmare, it usually takes longer to get back to sleep. Staying awake for the remainder of the night is more common. For those who are awakened by more than one nightmare each night, the average amount of sleep per night is usually small.

While lying in bed, PTSD patients often have a special problem. With the mind free to wander, they are apt to wander into their traumatic memory and rumination. When that happens, anxieties and tension escalate, making sleep difficult or impossible. The individual usually gets out of bed and tries to do something to divert attention, so that relaxation is once again possible. Falling asleep soon after a period of rumination makes nightmares more likely.

Another problem experienced by PTSD patients who are lying in bed is the tendency to listen for sounds, particularly sounds of danger.[21] Since it is easy to misinterpret sounds in the night, they can be another source of anxiety that keeps patients awake. For example, an acorn falling against the house or the groan of a tree in the wind are sounds that could elicit alarm. Patients may get out of bed repeatedly to check other rooms and look out of windows for signs of danger. Some PTSD patients say they can never sleep at night because of these problems, but can relax and get some sleep only during the day.

For those suffering from PTSD, quality of sleep is often poor, and they complain of not feeling rested in the morning. Many say they are restless during the night, thrash around in bed, and may fall out of bed. If that does not awaken them, some can continue sleeping on the floor. Many of these restless sleepers say they awaken with the sheets and blankets all twisted and out of place. This is apparently caused by nightmares that are not remembered.

Many PTSD patients awaken early and can't stay in bed. They arise an hour or two before it is time and may walk around or sit and drink coffee.

As indicated in the section on nightmares, many of those with PTSD have nightmares during the night they don't remember. It is possible that at least some of those who describe these symptoms of restless sleep are actually having nightmares repeatedly during the night.

Bruxism, or gritting and grinding the teeth during the night, is common for those with PTSD. It may occur most during nightmares, but is also apparently common when sleep is restless and the individual is tense. Some patients awaken with broken teeth when nightmares are severe, but breaking teeth is unusual with bruxism. Other dental problems are more common, including TMJ.

Chapter 15

"IRRITABILITY OR OUTBURSTS OF ANGER"

I rritability and temper are often the most troublesome symptoms for those suffering from PTSD.[22] Irritability is the tendency to get irritated over many things that happen during the day, even minor or small things. Patients often say they get terribly upset and angry over small, inconsequential things they would ordinarily pay no attention to. Afterwards they say, "It was nothing, it was stupid," or something similar to describe an overly determined reaction they later regret, and feel guilty about. The response is always out of proportion to the provocation, and happens instantly before the individual has a chance to think. Immediately afterwards the person usually feels remorse. Such events can occur many times each day, with an additive effect. The next reaction is apt to be even more explosive.

The outbursts of anger or temper are likewise apt to be quick and explosive, with regrets almost immediately afterwards in many instances. They often get so angry they fear harming or killing others. This degree of anger is a serious problem that sets PTSD patients apart. They may come to live in fear of something happening that will provoke the explosive temper. Anger is often a subject of discussion in PTSD groups. Many individuals have lost their temper at times and don't even remember what happened during a variable period of time, which makes the problem even more frightening. I have treated mothers who refuse to be alone with their children for fear of seriously hurting or even killing them. The prospect of losing control with explosive temper is frightening to everyone, and the possibility of not remembering afterwards is even more frightening.

Another unique aspect of the anger and temper problem is that individuals are often not aware of their anger, even when the degree is high. I have treated men who could not understand why everyone gets out of their way when they walk down a corridor. Others had experiences where a friend or relative feared for their life, even though the patient was completely unaware of the anger. Other individuals had problems

45

obtaining needed help in a hospital or clinic because they were not aware of behaving in a threatening and intimidating manner. When this problem exists, the individual must make it a priority to learn to recognize the anger. Efforts to control it are possible only after recognizing that it exists.

An example may help, since loss of control is such a serious problem. When loss of control is a possibility, PTSD patients are always advised to get rid of guns and other weapons. The reason is obvious, since sudden loss of control with a gun has lethal consequences. In one group, an individual had been talking about his concern over increasing anger at a family member. During a group meeting he mentioned that he still had one gun, unloaded, and had started glancing at the cabinet in which it was kept. Another group member who had long experience with temper problems said: "Get rid of that gun. One day you'll get mad at your relative, you've rehearsed in your mind just how you will reach for and load the gun. You'll blow him away and won't even remember it." This is powerful stuff. Needless to say, that group meeting was a particularly good one on the problems of coping with temper, and particularly helpful for the man with the problem.

Irritability and temper cause many marital and family problems. It is not unusual for men with PTSD to intimidate or physically assault their wives and children during fits of anger. This is one of the important reasons why divorces are common. In most instances, patients feel guilty after temper outbursts, but find it hard to control them. I have heard many men express regrets that their children were always afraid of them while growing up and would never get close. They feel strongly about "losing" their children and wish it could have been otherwise. Some individuals with PTSD become alienated from their entire family, including parents and siblings.

Irritability and temper also cause lots of problems with employment. The employee with PTSD is apt to have problems accepting supervision, gets angry at the boss or supervisor, reacts to someone watching, and is not tolerant of advice or corrections. Irritability also causes problems getting along with fellow employees. The individual often becomes isolated on the job, staying away from others to avoid incident. Working alone is often preferred. Irritability with supervisors leads to quitting jobs or getting fired. In some instances, supervisors are physically assaulted. Many PTSD patients have worked on numerous jobs, with few jobs lasting more than a few weeks or months. A work history like that can help make the diagnosis.

Persistent problems with irritability and temper lead many PTSD patients to a life of solitude. They prefer to stay away from people, rather than risk the problems that may occur with social contact. They move way out in the country, or stay at home or in their bedrooms most of the time. However, solitude and lack of activity tend to aggravate the problem of spending time with ruminations. This problem is often discussed during treatment.

Frequent, strong emotional reactions associated with irritability and temper, and the accompanying tension, often have physical consequences. For example, control of diabetes and epilepsy can be affected, as well as hypertension, cardiovascular problems, GI problems, and bruxism. Patients suffering PTSD symptoms over a period of years are likely to have some of these medical problems, and require a complete physical examination. These are additional reasons why control of this symptom is so important.

Another problem related to irritability and temper is frequent misdiagnosis. The behavior already described can easily be viewed as evidence for the diagnosis of personality disorder. The PTSD patient can be seen as a troublemaker in need of discipline, and the PTSD is usually not obvious. For example, this can be the problem when someone is discharged from military service with the diagnosis of personality disorder. The possibility of PTSD should be explored before the diagnosis of personality disorder is made, particularly with a past history of trauma.

Chapter 16

"DIFFICULTY CONCENTRATING"

When PTSD patients are spending time with and reliving a traumatic experience, it occupies their full concentration. As already discussed, this usually occurs without conscious recognition that it is occurring. When asked what they are thinking about at such times, patients will respond, "Nothing," since they are not consciously aware of the intrusive experience. Therefore, when the individual tries to read, comprehension is not possible, since we cannot concentrate fully on more than one thing at a time. Trying to watch TV is likewise a problem. The ruminating person can watch TV for an hour or two and have no idea of what programs were on, since concentration was elsewhere. Conversation involves similar problems.[23] The individual doesn't hear parts of what is said by another person. During a conversation, for example, patients may not remember what was said a moment or two ago, and may forget what they said themselves. The individual may try to converse, but loses the train of thought. It can be very frustrating, particularly because they lack conscious awareness of what is going on.

Preoccupation with ruminations causes the individual to forget appointments, meals, and medication. Family members must often help the patient with reminders. Left to their own devices, many patients would not remember to eat or take necessary medication. Since they forget so many things, they are painfully aware of memory problems. Such memory problems are usually associated with difficulty concentrating.

When questioning someone about symptoms of PTSD, they should be asked how long they can read. When closely questioned, many will admit they are often unable to read, or able to read for only a short time before losing concentration.

Inability to sustain concentration causes various problems in addition to those above. Failure in school and loss of jobs are common. Even though one is well qualified for a job, success is not possible. The individual is fired after a time, or quits before getting fired. Ability to earn a living may be impaired or lost, reducing self esteem.

Family and social life are also affected. The person who can't follow a conversation becomes self-conscious with others and starts avoiding people. This contributes to the tendency of many PTSD patients to isolate themselves from others, including family.

People with this problem are denied many pleasures they formerly enjoyed. For example, they may no longer be able to read a good book or watch a movie, or enjoy the company of family and friends.

Chapter 17

"HYPERVIGILANCE"

The symptom of hypervigilance is often described as being similar to the extremely alert state of the point man on a wartime patrol through the jungle. This individual is on guard and is relentlessly watchful and wary, looking for the slightest movement or listening for the faintest sound, and is ready to react instantly and vigorously to any possible threat. One with the symptom of hypervigilance is similarly watchful and wary at all times and in all situations. Those situations perceived as more threatening tend to heighten the level of vigilance. Walking down a dark street or alley would be an example. Other people getting physically close is often felt to be threatening, particularly if they are behind the individual. Shopping in crowded stores or malls is usually avoided by the hypervigilant patient, as well as standing in a line. When going into a restaurant, these patients will sit only with their backs to a corner or wall, in a place where they can watch the door in order to see who enters and leaves. Movie theaters are avoided because people can sit behind you. I have known some individuals with this symptom who can go to a movie theater if they sit in the last row.

Many PTSD patients have problems at home, particularly with children who come unexpectedly from behind. Since they can respond so instantly and vigorously before thinking, they are concerned about harming their children. They therefore warn family members repeatedly to avoid coming unexpectedly from behind. If approaching from behind them, they want family members to call out a warning before they get close.

The symptom of hypervigilance can restrict the patient's activities to various degrees, since many places and activities are avoided. There are those who are uncomfortable leaving the safety of their own home, and some become housebound. In some instances, individuals have difficulty leaving their bedroom, and may stay there for weeks or months at a time. These individuals are very uncomfortable even with family members.

In extreme cases, home becomes a military outpost, with defenses including guns, and positions that afford good view in all directions. Under such circumstances, confrontation with police can occur. That can obviously be dangerous. Fortunately, such problems are rare.

Since hypervigilance is usually directed toward threats from people, maintaining a safe distance from other people can become important. Some individuals therefore move far out in the country, to a home distant from other houses. As mentioned above, they may also set up a military type outpost from which approaching strangers can be seen before they get close. Occasionally this may include guns, fields of fire, and tripwires.

The hypervigilant individual feels threatened and uncomfortable whenever another person gets physically close. If the other person is a spouse or child, there is often a conflict between the desire to be close and loving, and the need to keep distance. Hypervigilance therefore appears to be involved in symptoms including *feeling of detachment or estrangement from others, or restricted range of affect, e.g., unable to have loving feelings.* This includes lack of sexual feelings and impotence.

Chapter 18

"EXAGGERATED STARTLE RESPONSE"

We are familiar with the example of a combat veteran who was the groom at a garden wedding. During the wedding ceremony, a passing truck backfired, causing him to dive instantly into the mud.

This is an example of the exaggerated startle response to a loud, usually unexpected sound. Sounds eliciting the response are often commonplace, like a shovel dropping to the garage floor, or a pot or dish dropped in the kitchen. Loud unexpected sounds that cause the problem may be specifically related to the trauma. Such sounds can include firecrackers, a particular (loud) voice, a starting motorcycle, the sudden roar of a helicopter, or the screech of tires on the pavement.

The startle response is not exactly the same for everyone. Some dive for cover, either onto the ground or under a table or other protection. This response is usually modified with time to the more common jump, a familiar body reaction to startle that can vary in degree.

Following the jump, or visible physical response, the individual starts hyperventilating, and is conscious of a pounding heart, anxiety, flushing, and possible additional symptoms related to anxiety. The person then tries to settle down by walking around, starting an activity, or simply resting. The length of time it takes to settle back down to normal can vary for each individual, depending on factors such as intensity of the startle response and how the individual was feeling before the startle. Some people can settle down in a few minutes at times, while on other occasions it could take an hour, or even several hours. Patients should be asked about how long it takes them to recover from a severe startle.

A severe startle can start the patient reliving a traumatic event. Therefore, symptoms of long duration after a startle can be caused or perpetuated by ruminations that the individual is not consciously aware of.

After a startle response, some individuals respond with anger, usually directed at the offending individual. After a severe startle response, the individual usually tries to identify the source of the sound. The person therefore looks around or may inquire of others. Identifying the source of the sound usually provides some relief. Inability to identify the source seems to leave one more troubled and tense.

Most people who have an obvious physical startle response are embarrassed by this and try to cover it up. It makes them more self-conscious, since they feel others laugh at them or look down on them for a behavior they are unable to control.

Ways to learn control of the startle response will be covered in the treatment section.

Chapter 19

"PHYSIOLOGIC REACTIVITY UPON EXPOSURE TO EVENTS THAT SYMBOLIZE OR RESEMBLE AN ASPECT OF THE TRAUMATIC EVENT (E.G., A WOMAN WHO WAS RAPED IN AN ELEVATOR BREAKS OUT IN A SWEAT WHEN ENTERING ANY ELEVATOR)"

Physiologic reactivity includes not only sweating, as above, but a number of other physiologic effects associated with anxiety and strong emotional stimuli. Included are cardiovascular changes, such as tachycardia, rhythm changes, extrasystoles, and abrupt change in blood pressure. Sudden lowering of blood pressure can cause fainting. Gastrointestinal effects may include spasm, pain, or diarrhea. Hyperventilation, muscle spasm, and skin reactions (hives) are additional possible physiologic effects.

Physiologic reactivity occurs upon exposure to specific situations or events, including situations resembling an aspect of the traumatic event. The above example of entering an elevator is clear and specific. However, the problem may occur in a situation not obviously related to the traumatic event. For example, an accident victim can have physiologic reactivity while walking or driving past an intersection not consciously recognized as resembling the location of the accident. The military veteran of a jungle war can experience the problem when walking in a park or garden that is not consciously recognized as resembling a combat area.

The physiologic reactivity is instantaneous and unanticipated. The individual is always taken by surprise, at least the first time. Subsequent exposures to a specific situation may then be anticipated. For instance, the woman entering an elevator in the above example will learn to expect the same reaction whenever she gets into an elevator, or she may simply use the stairs.

Chapter 20

DENIAL

As a consequence of centuries of lack of understanding and mis-information, people are usually stunned, frightened, overwhelmed, confused and ashamed of their normal emotions in response to trauma. They therefore cover up and hide the feelings and emotions they cannot accept in themselves. Living with these frightening and shameful emotions becomes difficult, particularly when symptoms of PTSD are prolonged.

Just as I could never admit to fear during combat or afterwards (I chose to risk death rather than make such an admission), everyone who experiences the normal reactions to trauma has the very strong need to deny the feelings, emotions, and consequent problems. Thinking or talking about the trauma is so upsetting that it is avoided if at all possible. Consequently, victims of trauma do not complain of symptoms or admit to problems. Most women who are raped, for example, never tell anyone because of these overwhelming feelings. For the macho male soldier or policeman, talking about this and admitting to feelings is even more difficult because feelings of manhood become involved.

The diagnosis of PTSD is therefore usually not made, since people won't come forth to talk about their symptoms, and they don't know that help is available. When interviewed, they do not volunteer information. When questioned, they will often deny symptoms. It is too difficult to deal with.

The key symptom of PTSD is ruminations, or the reexperiencing of a traumatic event. Since the individual is usually not consciously aware of the experience, the problem will be denied. This is true even for the person who is ruminating for many hours each day.

Making the diagnosis of PTSD usually requires perseverance and the ability to detect clues and follow them up, even in the face of denials.

Chapter 21

SUBSTANCE ABUSE

Victims of trauma who suffer symptoms of PTSD usually use and abuse substances that are available. I have known those traumatized in early childhood who began using alcohol or marijuana prior to adolescence. The combination of substance abuse and another diagnosis such as Dysthymia or PTSD is called *Dual Diagnosis.* [24]

There are logical reasons for the high frequency of substance abuse associated with PTSD.[25] First, the powerful feelings of shame and inadequacy resulting from a normal response to trauma become difficult to live with and can't be shared with another human being. The individual feels alone and isolated, and shuts off help from others.

As PTSD symptoms develop, time with ruminations increases. Since the traumatic experience is relived each time with the full emotional intensity of the original trauma, and may be reexperienced many times daily, the intensity of suffering is high and intolerable. Since help from others cannot be considered, substance abuse often appears to be the only source of relief.

I have known many PTSD patients who abused alcohol or other drugs for a period of years and then stopped. At some point they recognized, or were helped to recognize, that it was not the answer, and that they were harming themselves. I have also known individuals who are unable to stop, and who view substances as their only dependable source of help and relief.

Many individuals enter detoxification programs repeatedly and are considered to be addicts or alcoholics.[26] The underlying PTSD often goes unrecognized. However, it is clear that treatment for dual diagnosis is indicated, underlining the importance of making the diagnosis of PTSD. The PTSD must be treated along with the substance abuse. There are now many fine programs that accomplish this very well.

Some individuals develop hallucinations and delusions from drugs. Since they are manifesting the symptoms of schizophrenia, in the hospital they are usually given the diagnosis of schizophrenia, a diagnosis they may carry for years or for a lifetime. They are therefore treated for schizophrenia, rather than substance abuse and PTSD.

Since the risk for substance abuse is high for juveniles with PTSD, early detection and treatment are important. Here again accurate diagnosis is the key.

Chapter 22

DEPRESSION

Everyone with PTSD suffers from depression.[27] Although the depression may be covered up and not obvious, it is more often severe depression, with crying and a full range of depressive symptoms that can include suicidal ideation and suicide attempts.

Depression is associated with the shame and stigma regarding feelings and symptoms, as already described. Depression also results from the suffering associated with ruminations, inability to communicate with other human beings about the problem, and feeling after a time that no relief is possible or forthcoming. Another source of depression is guilt (including self-blame, survivor guilt), which is likewise always associated with PTSD. Physical problems (and pain), sleep problems, and fatigue also add to the depression. In addition, there is often guilt toward family about temper, social withdrawal, and inability to be close and loving, inability to earn a living, guilt about substance abuse, and guilt about various other symptoms.[28]

Crying is common and is particularly embarrassing for men. I have known war veterans who walk around with tears streaming down their cheeks, or who started crying whenever they tried to speak during group therapy. The tolerance and understanding of other group members is very therapeutic when this occurs, and the problem gradually diminishes.

When depressive symptoms are prominent, the diagnosis of Dysthymia is often made, and at times Major Depression.[29] I have known many PTSD patients who were treated for depression for a number of years. The depressive symptoms are more effectively treated when the underlying diagnosis of PTSD is also treated.

Chapter 23

CRYING

Most people who are depressed do some crying, and most PTSD patients are depressed. However, the crying of PTSD patients has some special qualities.

The crying PTSD patient, on average, does more crying for a longer period of time than the crying depressed patient. It can go on for many months, even years. I have known many PTSD patients who keep crying much of the day and complain that they cry "for every little thing." I have seen men in groups cry much or most of the time during group therapy. Things they hear in group may make them cry more. If they stop crying and try to speak, they can't because they start crying again. In some instances it can take several months of treatment before the crying diminishes. Crying like this without control can be frustrating to the patient, and men tend to be more embarrassed about it than women.

Another statement I often hear from PTSD patients is, "I cry for no reason." They complain of starting to cry out of the blue at unexpected times and during various activities. They are not aware of feeling depressed at these times, and usually say that nothing happened that would account for the crying. The crying can occur many times each day, and last for a variable period of time. Patients often complain of becoming embarrassed when it occurs in social situations. This symptom therefore contributes to the tendency of PTSD patients to avoid social contact.

Another common characteristic is that tears can be streaming down the cheeks, without the individual being aware of it. It is possible that the lack of awareness results from preoccupation with ruminations, which may have caused the crying.

I continue to see many combat veterans in PTSD groups. Some of them have friends still on active duty on the nearby military reservation. In the months following return of troops from the Gulf War, they reported frequently seeing soldiers walking along the street with tears streaming down their cheeks.

Chapter 24

ANXIETY, PANIC

The individual suffering from PTSD slips into reexperiencing the traumatic event without conscious awareness. The result of spending time with intensely disturbing emotions includes symptoms already reviewed. These symptoms and upsets can strike suddenly, and appear to come from nowhere and without reason, since there is no conscious awareness of the rumination. Symptoms may include the full range of anxiety symptoms, or only some of them. They include anxiety, apprehension, worry, feeling keyed up or on edge, with irritability, difficulty concentrating, and exaggerated startle response. Autonomic hyperactivity associated with anxiety can involve shortness of breath, smothering sensations, palpitations, sweating or cold clammy hands, dry mouth, dizziness, flushes or chills, trouble swallowing, GI effects like nausea and diarrhea, and frequent urination. Motor tension includes muscle tension and pain, trembling or feeling shaky, and restlessness.

Since intense anxiety can appear suddenly and without warning or apparent reason when one has slipped into ruminations, the diagnosis of *Panic Disorder* is often made. The essential features of this disorder include discrete periods of intense fear or discomfort that are unexpected, usually last minutes, but can sometimes last longer. During such an episode, the individual can have chest pain, fear of dying, and fear of going crazy, in addition to the above symptoms of anxiety. PTSD patients often experience this entire set of problems. However, the PTSD patient also has a history of trauma, and many other symptoms related to that diagnosis.

With both Panic Disorder and PTSD, therefore, the individual may come to live in fear of the next attack because of the high level of distress and also because of the unpredictability of the next occurrence. This stress and apprehension can therefore serve to bring on the dreaded symptoms.

I have known many PTSD patients who were treated over the years for an anxiety or panic disorder. This is understandable, since PTSD patients so often suffer from these symptoms, are unable to talk about their trauma, and are not aware of ruminations. When evaluating a patient with these symptoms, therefore, the possibility of PTSD should always be considered. On many occasions I have made the diagnosis of PTSD for patients who were previously treated for Anxiety Disorder or Panic Disorder.

Chapter 25

MOST COMFORTABLE WHEN ALONE

Almost all PTSD patients are uncomfortable with people and many say they are most comfortable when alone. It is common for them to have difficulty leaving the house because of their problems with facing and dealing with people. Some PTSD patients become housebound, and some of those even have difficulty leaving their bedroom. They prefer to avoid even other family members. Some individuals move far out in the country and prefer a location that is far from another human being. The frequency and intensity of social discomfort appears to be higher than in any other diagnostic category.

We can only speculate about the reasons for this problem. In part, it seems to be related to the symptom of hypervigilance. These patients have trouble trusting others, and staying as far away as possible from potential sources of danger would fit with hypervigilance. For many, their traumatic experience was more traumatic because they were close to someone else when it occurred, or they were injured or abused by another person, so keeping distance could be viewed as defensive and protective. Strong feelings of stigma could also relate to this symptom.

Discomfort with others often causes family and marital problems for the PTSD patient. A spouse will resent being left with responsibility for raising the children and for household needs. Children will resent the parent who stays locked in the bedroom. PTSD patients who mistrust others and can't get close are usually not interested in love and sex, another frustration for the spouse. This symptom therefore contributes to the high rate of marital problems and divorce associated with the diagnosis of PTSD.

The PTSD patient who is working may have job problems related to this symptom. Getting along with fellow employees may be difficult. The patient may get distracted when others get close, and may have arguments and fights at work. Jobs are often lost for this reason. I am familiar with many instances in which PTSD patients finally got a job assignment in which they could work alone, at some distance from others, and often in a completely separate room. They are often valued employees who can do a good job if arrangements can be made to keep them away from other people.

Chapter 26

DISSOCIATIVE EXPERIENCES

As previously described, the PTSD patient often drifts unrecognized into reexperiencing the trauma. Reliving a traumatic experience in this manner occupies the person's full attention. What is going on in the room or on the TV is therefore not registering. Someone can therefore sit watching TV for an hour or more and remember nothing of what was seen or heard. A frustrated wife may say, "You didn't hear a word I said," or "You're not here. Where are you?" Since even large parts of a conversation may not register, the individual can have difficulty holding a simple conversation. Some individuals go in and out for varying periods, and therefore get bits and pieces of a conversation or whatever is going on.

The average person experiences a similar problem, but to a much lesser degree. While driving some distance on an interstate highway, for example, the individual may be suddenly aware of the town being passed and not remember passing the previous town or city. While preoccupied, people also occasionally pass their exit. These brief memory lapses are not usually cause for concern by most people, even though they can be annoying.

Unlike the average person, the PTSD patient has longer and more frequent episodes of preoccupation.[30] Upon return to full awareness, and recognition that there was a blank period of time, the patient is often concerned about what happened during that episode. Patients often say things like, "I could have killed somebody," or, "I could have run over somebody with my car," or similar expressions of deep concern. There is always complete amnesia for the entire period of time.[31]

Duration of these episodes is quite variable for PTSD patients.[32] They are apt to have longer and more frequent such periods than the average person while driving the highway, usually with some degree of concern about what might have happened during the period of amnesia. "I could have killed somebody," is a concern that is fairly frequently heard during group therapy regarding these episodes.

Some episodes can last a full day or up to several days or more.[33] The PTSD patient can come to awareness in a strange location, or in a city hundreds of miles away. This is always most upsetting, and gives rise to concerns about how they got there, what happened along the way, and what they might have done during that time. Serious concerns and guilt like this can weigh heavily on the individual.

These episodes tend to begin when one is drowsy or sleeping, and possibly could be the continuation of a nightmare. I recall one individual who last recalls lying down to rest on a recliner one afternoon. He spent a few days fishing at a nearby lake, sleeping in his tent. His family came there looking for him, and he does not remember talking to them. One morning he suddenly said, "How did I get here," and proceeded to go home. He had no memory of the entire period. The last thing he remembered was resting on his recliner. PTSD patients often report resting during the day preceding an extended dissociative episode for which they have complete amnesia, suggesting that it started either while they were drowsy, or following a nightmare.

A patient may remain at home and lose a day or two in this manner. The problem is often referred to as *losing time.* A spouse may relate that the individual was on the couch or in bed most of the time. I have known patients who remained in one position for more than twenty-four hours without moving, not even to go to the bathroom. They get very concerned when hearing this from family, since there is no memory for the entire block of time. There are additional concerns when someone has a medical condition like diabetes or a heart condition that requires daily doses of medication.

I suspect that during these dissociative episodes, PTSD patients are spending at least some of the time reliving traumatic memories. However, I know of no way to verify that.

Dissociative symptoms are often related to traumatic experiences.[34] A good example is the battle-weary soldier who may no longer relate to date, time of day, to others in his unit, or even to the threat of injury and death. He can be detached from his usual feelings and emotions about these things for various periods of time.

For patients suffering from PTSD, there can be a return at times to some of the dissociative events related to their original trauma. For example, in a particular situation, an individual can suddenly feel detached, things seem strange and may move in slow motion, the area and even family members can look strange and different.

This description of a dissociative event raises an important question. When an individual faced with a particular situation has such a reaction, could it be related to a rumination that was triggered by the situation? If so, the dissociative symptom described would be part of the rumination experience, rather than a separate symptom. I am inclined to believe this.

We have described activity after a nightmare, which may be a continuation of the nightmare or somehow related to the nightmare. These periods of activity are usually considered to be dissociative. They vary in duration, and the episode may terminate when the individual becomes fully awake.

Chapter 27

GUILT

There is always guilt[35] related to the traumatic experience. There are different aspects of the guilt problem, and an individual may have all or only some of these.

The victim tends to blame self. This can be true of the rape victim, who often feels that she somehow did something to provoke the rape and is therefore responsible. The war veteran can feel responsible for the death of his friend because he should have done something that would have prevented the death.

In my own experience with this problem, I thought back to the death of a number of my friends. In each instance, I would think of an action on my part that would have prevented their death. I then felt guilty for not having done something different, and that I was therefore responsible for the death of each of my friends. The burden was difficult to bear.

Fortunately, I gradually figured out the problem. I recognized that hindsight is always much more accurate, and that I was being unfair to myself. I always did the best I could in combat, and realized that doing my best is all I can do. The fact that my best did not save my friends was due to enemy fire and the misfortunes of war, not to my lack of effort. They were killed by the enemy, not by me. I was not responsible for their death. Reminding myself of these facts over and over gradually helped solve the problem over a period of time.

In some instances, individuals have unintentionally killed a friend or a loved one. For example, it could happen when a gun goes off accidentally or when someone is accidentally hit by a car. In every war soldiers are shot by mistake for various reasons. A soldier can also shoot his friend who is burning up or just had a large hole shot through his chest, in order to decrease pain and suffering before death. He may also kill a friend who has suddenly gone berserk and started shooting at or otherwise endangering the entire unit. Afterwards comes the guilt and questions about having done the right thing. These are some of the most disturbing guilts, and the most difficult to forget or to talk about. Individuals who consider themselves murderers in this manner are apt to be more depressed, more self-critical, and to feel themselves even less deserving of consideration or respect.

There is usually some distortion of memories over a period of time. It rarely happened exactly the way we remember. The memory distortion of a traumatic memory tends to be in the direction of greater guilt, increasing the intensity of guilt. For example, in group therapy with combat veterans, an individual may relate a combat event in which he feels responsible for the death of others. Group members often refute the concerns, or give reasonable and objective reasons why the individual is not responsible. I sat in one group meeting in which a guilt-ridden individual advised a direction for the patrol to go that resulted in an explosion killing everyone but him. Peer questioning revealed, for example, that privates don't lead patrols and make the decisions on where to go, so the decision wasn't his to make. In addition, group members verified the direction for the patrol by saying things like, "Under those conditions, that's the way I would go." The fact that others were killed going that way is in the nature of war, since it is impossible to predict with certainty the results of any such decision. You know only afterwards if the decision was correct, even though you make your best judgment at the time.

The latter example also illustrates the problem of *survivor guilt.* The survivor asks, "Why me and not them?" If a friend is killed in combat, for example, the individual will ask, "Why him and not me?", or, "He was married with two children and I was single." After any disaster, such as train wrecks, storms, or vehicle accidents, survivors tend to feel guilty and troubled by similar questions. Consequently, survivor guilt is common with PTSD.

At least some survivor guilt may be caused or increased by a natural and very human reaction related to self preservation. In the face of danger, we all secretly hope that we will survive, that if anything happens, it will be to the other person. We also feel guilty about such feelings. When death claims the other person, we then feel even more guilty because the forbidden wish is fulfilled, and we feel somehow responsible.

The self-blame and guilt usually associated with PTSD adds to the reluctance of people to talk about their problem, and also contributes to depression.

Chapter 28

PROBLEMS WITH MEMORY

Various problems with memory[36] tend to be associated with PTSD. For some reason, memory problems were included in *DSM-III* but were not listed in *DSM-III-R*.

Most problems with memory appear to be related to ruminations, which can be intrusive, frequent, and long lasting. Difficulty concentrating and difficulty remembering are therefore related problems. While one is reexperiencing the traumatic event, there is no awareness of what is going on in the room. The individual will not respond to questions, and is unaware of the TV program. They may look like they hear what you say, but they don't. A person with this problem is not aware of what is happening at the moment and is unable to say where the mind was wandering. Ruminations appear to somehow disrupt the process of memory, apparently because attention and train of thought are frequently interrupted.

For older patients with PTSD, age tends to be the reason given for poor memory.[37] However, I have known many fairly young PTSD patients who have similar problems. They complain, for example, that when they go to the store, they can't remember what they went for. They can even walk to another room and forget what they went for. Many forget to eat their meals or take medication regularly, and when asked, can't recall if or when they took the medication. For this reason, a spouse or family member will often remind the patient about medication, meals, or appointments.

PTSD patients often miss their appointments unless a family member reminds them. For this reason, I phone many of my patients an hour or two before the appointment, or early in the morning if they are apt to leave the house early. I have often called individuals who were alone at home, ruminating. They answer the phone and sound like they were awakened from deep sleep. The phone call helps them pull themselves away from the ruminating and get out for the appointment.

Chapter 29

PHYSICAL AND MEDICAL PROBLEMS

I have already described the high degree of stress associated with ruminations and reexperiencing the traumatic event for the PTSD patient. In recent years, the physical and medical effects of severe and long-lasting stress has been documented in many publications.[38] All organs and organ systems may become involved.[39]

One study, for example, demonstrated a degree of myocardial ischemia (reduced circulation to heart muscle) induced by performance of a simple arithmetic task. Another demonstrated that stress and related excessive sympathetic activity may cause myocardial damage, disordered cardiac rhythms, and sudden death. Other studies document the relationship of stress to gastrointestinal, musculoskeletal and headache problems, and even to diabetes mellitus.

While working for the Veterans Administration over a period of years, it became obvious that the PTSD group of patients had a much higher incidence of physical and medical problems[40] than the veterans who saw no combat. Because of reluctance to expose any type of problem, they often suffered severe physical symptoms (including pain) for a number of years before finally requesting medical evaluation. Many group members had hypertension, cardiac problems,[41] history of bypass surgery, and saw a cardiologist regularly. Gastrointestinal problems[42] were likewise common, with a high incidence of GI surgery and the need for medication. Orthopedic and musculoskeletal problems were also common, as well as bruxism (grinding the teeth during sleep). Many group members therefore had dental problems including TMJ pain. Since I feel that all physical and medical problems require evaluation and competent treatment, I worked closely with other medical specialists, particularly because many of my patients were taking antidepressants that can affect the dose of other medicines.

Many physical symptoms related to stress appear to be reversible. Most regular group members reported reduced symptoms and pain over a period of time. In many instances, the required dose of medication for a medical problem was reduced. The physical improvements related to PTSD treatment were often remarkable. When the subject came up in group therapy, a common comment was, "I would have been dead without this treatment."

We previously reviewed the reluctance of PTSD patients to talk about or admit to their symptoms. Therefore, the first doctor they see is likely to hear about physical complaints, like pain in the chest or abdomen. All physical symptoms require appropriate evaluation and treatment. In the process, the primary physician should be alert to the possibility of PTSD.

Chapter 30

PARANOID THINKING

Paranoid thinking and behavior is common for those suffering from PTSD.[43] Some individuals can't trust anyone, either to be physically close or to treat them fairly in a business transaction or in personal matters. Such suspicions can apply to family, including spouse and children. If some money or time can't be accounted for, a spouse will be accused of running around. Ulterior motives are quickly suspected regarding even small matters. This problem adds to the disruption of family relationships and the high rate of marital problems and divorce. Friendships can be terminated abruptly because of suspicions and accusations. This adds further to the social isolation of many with PTSD who can't feel comfortable with anyone, or in some cases can't even leave the home. Work adjustment is likewise affected. The diagnosis of schizophrenia, paranoid type, is sometimes made.[44]

Paranoid thinking can contribute to the severity of other symptoms, including avoidance, diminished interest in significant activities, feelings of detachment or estrangement, irritability and temper, difficulty concentrating, hypervigilance, social isolation, and substance abuse. This aspect of each symptom must be explored.

For some, there is selective trust or mistrust. For example, a woman who has been raped or abused by men may be fairly comfortable with women but on guard with all men. She may mistrust what they say, their motives, and may be unable to get physically close. She may become very uncomfortable if a man comes within several feet of her.

The paranoid problem can manifest itself in treatment in various ways. For example, an abused woman can have difficulty in working with a male therapist. Some individuals refuse group therapy because they can't tolerate other people or groups of people, either because of mistrust, inability to tolerate the physical proximity, or both.

An example of change in this behavior comes from a PTSD group of Vietnam veterans. Some individuals say they can relax only in the group, where they are surrounded by fellow combat veterans. At such times they may not be uncomfortable with someone physically close or even behind them. This may be the only situation in which they feel comfortable. I have known some who doze off during group meetings. They are apologetic, and explain that they doze because this is the only place they can really relax. I could provide many other examples of selective trust and mistrust, which usually depends on the specific trauma involved.

Chapter 31

WORKAHOLIC TENDENCIES,
OVERCOMPENSATION

People suffering from PTSD may spend many years with serious problems. This is true, as already discussed, because of the difficulty in recognizing the problem, either by the patient or by professionals, and because of denial. Even though many individuals are completely unaware of triggers, ruminations, and resulting problems, most become aware with time that certain things seem to make them more uncomfortable while others help.

Therefore, it is common to meet individuals with PTSD who work two and even three jobs. They recognize that working, which provides tasks needing concentration, seems to help. With this is also an awareness of increased discomfort when not working, since the mind is more free to wander. In addition, many of these individuals choose to get so physically exhausted that they get some sleep when finally going to bed. They often say that if not exhausted, they lie in bed, get nervous, and can't sleep at all. Physical outlets and fatigue seem to be helpful.

I have met many individuals who worked two or more jobs for a number of years before learning that they had PTSD. Since they see little of their family, family and marital relationships suffer. This contributes to a high divorce rate. Since friends are also neglected, social isolation is common. This symptom is therefore related to the symptom of avoidance. As one gets older and less able to sustain the pace of physical effort and long hours, symptoms begin to increase. Issues like this must often be dealt with in marital therapy.

Overcompensation is a related issue that is usually seen in those with disability, whether physical or emotional. Disabled people tend to be very self-conscious about their disability, and feel a stigma that results in feelings of difference and inferiority. Overcompensation and the need to excel is a common response to such feelings.

First I will give examples of overcompensation from my own experience. One of my war injuries resulted in a fused knee, so there is one solid bone from hip to ankle. I was self-conscious about walking with a limp, and felt the need to demonstrate my physical prowess in various ways. On the street I would try to walk faster than anyone else. It took a number of years for me to realize that the people I passed while walking did not really notice or even care. It was entirely within me. I was trying to prove something to myself. I even started to ski before I realized I was at much greater risk for injury and it was a dumb thing to do. In school I was also driven to excel, and was never happy with an average grade. I felt I had to be the best and have the highest grades. Obviously, these behaviors are determined by emotions and have nothing to do with intelligence.

Overcompensation may therefore be a factor in PTSD patients with workaholic problems, since they are troubled by feelings of stigma. It could be a way of demonstrating superiority to others who have only one job or who work regular hours. Many PTSD patients have physical disabilities that add to the feelings of stigma. An individual who is doing well with career and family may therefore be the envy of many. However, if this individual is driven to overcompensate, accomplishments are derogated because they must do more or better. No level of achievement will be satisfying or good enough because of the feeling that it should be even better. There are degrees of this problem, and changes take place gradually and by degree. It is necessary to deal with feelings of stigma and also feelings of inferiority in order to help this problem.

Chapter 32

COURTING DANGER: THE ADRENALIN HIGH

Those suffering from PTSD often give a history of courting danger. Those in the police or the military keep asking for the most dangerous assignments. Many others take unusual risks, from mountain and rock climbing to jumping out of airplanes and racing on the street or cross country. A small man may challenge bigger men to fight. Some try drugs that are potentially lethal. A few will speed up when they see a police car to provoke a chase. These are but a few examples. When talking about it, these people often say things like, "I don't know why I do that," or, "I don't know what got into me."

I do not want to imply that every policeman or mountain climber who is willing to take risks suffers from PTSD. Most of them don't. However, when a PTSD patient has this symptom, courting danger is common. The individual who reacts to danger in this way is not consciously aware of the reason for their reaction. The problem is usually recognized during treatment for PTSD.

Understanding of this behavior can probably be helped by reviewing some typical events from childhood. Many children enjoy frightening rides, like the roller coaster. Many also enjoy frightening movies. We may continue to enjoy these things as we get older. The question is why anyone would enjoy being frightened. It should be an unpleasant experience. However, although unpleasant for some, it is pleasant and enjoyable for a high percentage of people.

The answer appears to be the *high* that often accompanies the adrenalin rush. This is experienced as exhilerating, pleasant, and enjoyable. Therefore, the adrenalin rush may be sought repeatedly.

PTSD patients have had frightening experiences, usually more frightening than the above examples. Many of these patients have suffered repeated trauma over a period of time, each event associated with high adrenalin levels. For some, the rush of adrenalin becomes enjoyable. Individuals in military combat may do things or volunteer for missions in order to induce the adrenalin high. I have heard veterans describe this as, "Feeling good, you are more alert, have surprising strength, you can do anything." They also say things like, "If you could bottle it, it would put all the other drugs out of business." It is clearly perceived as an addiction to the adrenalin rush, with risk taking behavior to achieve a high.

PTSD patients who have suffered repeated trauma are more likely to have this problem. In therapy, therefore, individuals must learn to identify ways in which they provoke risk and danger so control is possible. They learn to recognize how such behavior causes many life problems, and how efforts toward change are beneficial.

Chapter 33

PROFOUND CHANGES

The onset of PTSD is often associated with profound changes in the individual. The changes may include personality, behavior, and lifestyle. Family and friends are often astounded by the degree of change and will say things like, "You are not the same person." If they are aware that the individual experienced a trauma, they do not relate that to the changes they observe.

For example, someone who was formerly very sociable and outgoing can start avoiding people and remain at home alone in their room. Someone who was formerly affable and easy to get along with can become irritable over the slightest thing and have a bad temper. Someone who was formerly loving and close to spouse and children can become distant, avoid getting close, and appear cold and uncaring. Someone who never used alcohol or other drugs can suddenly start abusing them. These are but a few examples of changes that can occur. For any individual, one or several such changes can occur, and the changes can be moderate or severe and abrupt.

A person's entire life or lifestyle can drastically change. For no apparent reason, the individual can leave job and home, even though they were previously considered reliable and dependable. In some instances, such a person could abandon family and become an addict living on the streets.

Unexpected changes like those described can be caused by PTSD that the individual has been unable to talk about or deal with or has not even been aware of. The diagnosis should therefore be suspected when changes occur that are difficult to understand. This is true for children and adolescents, who may become socially uncomfortable, moody, hard to get along with, aggressive, and start to get poor grades in school. The youngster who suddenly starts using alcohol or other drugs may be suffering from PTSD.

A common type of change in personality for those with PTSD relates to the symptom of irritability and temper. Someone who was formerly mild mannered can become irritable, argumentative, even threatening or violent. Family members can come to fear them. They come to be known as troublemakers on the job and may get fired or quit. In addition, if a medical or psychiatric examination is requested, the diagnosis of Antisocial Personality Disorder or Borderline Personality Disorder may be made. This is at times a problem in organizations like the police and the military. The soldier suffering from PTSD who is discharged from the Army with the diagnosis of Antisocial Personality Disorder, for example, loses retirement benefits and medical benefits, and his problem goes untreated.

Chapter 34

PTSD IN FAMILY MEMBERS

Family members living with a PTSD patient usually develop symptoms of PTSD to some degree.[45] Spouse and children are usually most affected.

Concerns can start even before the exposure to danger, when the family knows that the individual will face danger, injury, or death. For example, a military wife who learns that her husband will be sent to a war zone can start visualizing him blown up, crashing in a plane, or otherwise injured or killed. She can start having ruminations of such events, along with other PTSD symptoms, and develop the full PTSD syndrome. This can occur with the spouse and children of police, firefighters, and many others who have dangerous jobs.

Family members living daily with one who suffers from PTSD symptoms also tend to develop similar symptoms. Since they are all familiar with the trauma involved, they can, like the patient, start having ruminations and nightmares. Other symptoms may come to be included, such as anxiety, depression, and social discomfort. When the patient has symptoms of irritability and temper, family members can also develop those symptoms. Likewise, children who observe hypervigilance in one of their parents may also become watchful and remain on guard.

This process leads to various family complications. For example, if both husband and wife have temper problems, marital discord escalates. Children can become upset, school grades can go down, and they may even get into drugs.

Since family members are always involved, adequate treatment for PTSD must include family therapy. Specifics about involving family in treatment will be discussed in a later section.

Chapter 35

FAMILY AND MARITAL PROBLEMS

Family and marital problems are usually associated with PTSD.[46] The problems that can disrupt marriages and families result from specific symptoms of the disorder.

Ruminations can keep the patient away from family interaction when many hours each day are spent "someplace else, not here." Therefore, for example, a wife can feel that she doesn't have a husband most of the time and can't depend on him. Children are also confused by a father who is withdrawn much of the time and who may do frightening things.

Nightmares can be a family problem when the patient starts screaming during the night. They are frightened by the partially asleep patient who continues to relive an experience at night and threatens to be assaultive and destructive. A spouse can be injured in bed during these episodes, and may decide to sleep in another room.

The symptoms of detachment, estrangement, and inability to have love feelings certainly impact the family. Children can be frightened by a father who cannot feel close to them. Impotence and loss of sexual feelings and interest tend to impair the marital relationship.

Irritability and temper often impact family and marital relationships in a serious manner. The patient can flare with a terrible temper unexpectedly at times and not remember the episode, frightening the family. A wife gets frustrated when she can't deal with her husband without fear of a temper outburst or even physical attack. Children avoid a parent they fear, and can come to hate such a parent.

Since substance abuse is also common for PTSD patients, the above problems are further complicated. Effects of substance abuse include prolonged absences from home and family, increased frequency and intensity of ruminations, increase of detachment and impotence, and increased frequency and intensity of irritability and temper.

A number of other PTSD symptoms may contribute to family and marital problems. They include hypervigilance, depression, most comfortable when alone, dissociative experiences, paranoid thinking, and workaholic tendencies.

Family and marital therapy are therefore an essential aspect of treatment for PTSD. Family members are confused by the changes in their loved one and don't understand many of the changes and unfamiliar behaviors. They are also usually frightened and angry. They are therefore relieved to get answers and accurate information. Without family therapy, families often break up. PTSD patients also need the help of their family in the process of treatment and recovery.

Chapter 36

MULTIPLE MARRIAGE AND DIVORCE

The prevalence of family and marital problems for PTSD patients is caused by various symptoms of the disorder, as already reviewed. After a time, the patient tends to feel persecuted and picked on unfairly at home. With this, the patient usually fails to recognize how he or she provokes the criticism and anger, and gets angry in return. Divorce is therefore common. It is not unusual to meet PTSD patients who have had three to five marriages, and for some it is seven or eight marriages and divorces. Children from previous marriages may further complicate later marriages.

Therefore, if a patient has a history of multiple marriages and divorces, the diagnosis of PTSD should be considered.

Chapter 37

STRONG REACTION TO ANGER AND VIOLENCE

As a group, PTSD patients have usually been exposed to more than the average amount of violence. This is particularly true of those experiencing violence repeatedly over a period of time. Examples are children who were abused over a period of years, combat veterans, and ex-POWs.

Most PTSD patients therefore react more strongly than average to violence of any type, so movies and TV shows portraying violence are usually avoided. These movie portrayals may arouse strong feelings, probably because they trigger the start of ruminations. The fact that they are triggers apparently accounts, at least in part, for the strength of these reactions. I have known individuals who became so angry while watching TV that they smashed the TV or even threw it out the window.

Loud disagreements between others that carry the possibility of leading to violence are another example. Some PTSD patients therefore start feeling uncomfortable when hearing almost any verbal disagreement. This can apply to political disagreements, and particularly to issues of military intervention or threats of war. Patients can get worked up and even very angry over things like this.

I can give examples from my own past experience. Even though I knew young children can disagree and even fight briefly at times, I would react strongly to fighting among my children. On one occasion a child was crying from what I assumed to be aggression from an older sibling. I quickly started shouting angrily at the older child, and later felt guilty to learn that I had made a mistake. The older child was trying to be helpful rather than aggressive, but I allowed no time for explanation.

Chapter 38

INTOLERANCE OF STRESS

S tress appears to have more than the average effect on those suffering from PTSD. As indicated in previous sections, stress appears to trigger ruminations, so that the individual under stress spends additional time reliving traumatic experiences. Stress from any source seems to be a trigger, whether or not it is related in some way to the trauma. The stress could be financial problems, marital problems, severe pain, the list is endless. Spending more time ruminating and reliving traumatic events increases symptoms including anxiety, depression, and the various other symptoms of PTSD. Hypertension and various other physical symptoms may also increase.

Even though not aware of ruminations, the patient learns to avoid stress if at all possible. The patient who refuses to leave the house is avoiding, among other things, the stress of dealing with people and events that could be encountered. Limiting activities of any kind could represent, at least in part, an attempt to reduce or avoid stress that would increase ruminations.

Intolerance of stress often becomes a work and training issue. I have often heard individuals relate how they chose a job with lower pay in order to work away from others, or in a department with lower stress. PTSD patients often leave jobs because of inability to tolerate the stress of the job.

When the PTSD patient applies for placement, counseling, or training for a new job, the factor of stress must be considered. I generally suggest that PTSD patients avoid high stress jobs and training. Examples include highly competitive or hectic work environments that are typical in certain fields. Some work environments feature constant pressure for production. Therefore, avoiding stressful work environments such as these can help the PTSD patient achieve a successful job adjustment.

Chapter 39

TIPS FOR MAKING THE DIAGNOSIS
MORE CONSISTENTLY

PTSD can resemble a variety of diagnoses, as already reviewed. In addition, the diagnosis is difficult to make because the patient doesn't volunteer information about it, and often denies symptoms. When evaluating a patient, it can therefore help if one is familiar with symptoms that are fairly specific for PTSD. These specifics have previously been described under individual symptoms. Although individual symptoms may be clues that alert one to the possibility of PTSD, diagnosis must be made on the basis of a combination of symptoms. Since PTSD is so common and so frequently overlooked, clues can alert the examiner to search for additional symptoms.

Changes in the individual's behavior, functioning, and adjustment generally indicate a problem.[47] Although PTSD is not the only diagnosis indicated by such changes, it should always be considered. Additionally, PTSD can accompany other diagnoses, including schizophrenia, bipolar disorder, and substance abuse.[48] Diminished interest in significant activities is one of the listed symptoms of PTSD, and represents one type of change that can alert the examiner.

Relatives may report that the individual is often preoccupied and seems to be elsewhere even though the patient is not aware of it. This behavior may indicate ruminations, with the person reliving a traumatic event. Social withdrawal often accompanies this, since the PTSD patient prefers to be alone.

The onset of frightening dreams and nightmares may also be a symptom of PTSD. Associated with nightmares can be awakening in the morning somewhere other then in bed. This appears to be specific for PTSD, as does getting up during the night and doing things that are not remembered in the morning.

The symptom of avoidance can be indicated by changes in where one will or won't go, and changes in activities. An extreme degree of this problem is represented by the individual becoming housebound, and in some instances, by a refusal to leave the bedroom. There are instances in which a person has remained in one bedroom for years. I talked recently to someone who has an uncle who is a World War II veteran. She recalls that over the years he always stayed in his bedroom. That is her only memory of him, and he apparently suffers from PTSD.

Sudden onset of marital problems in a previously stable marriage can be caused by PTSD symptoms such as detachment, inability to have loving feelings, loss of interest in sex, and sexual impotence. PTSD usually causes marital problems, and they are often serious. A high rate of divorce and remarriage may be associated with PTSD.

Irritability and temper may accompany other conditions, such as depression. However, an extreme degree of temper is more typical of PTSD. When one is afraid of losing control and actually killing others, the diagnosis of PTSD is more likely. For example, a woman who becomes afraid of staying home alone with her children for this reason is likely to be suffering from PTSD. Temper is also the cause of much marital discord for PTSD patients.

The symptom of hypervigilance has qualities specific for PTSD. The individual becomes watchful, keeps distance from others, and is particularly sensitive about anyone coming up from behind. PTSD patients often refuse to stand in lines, since in line someone is always behind you. In a room or restaurant, they usually must sit with their back to a wall or corner where they can watch the door. A patient should therefore be asked about preferred seating location in a restaurant. A spouse can readily answer this question.

Dissociative experiences often occur with PTSD, and PTSD is possibly the most common cause of such experiences. The individual can suddenly *wake up* and not know what has happened for the past couple of hours or days. Survivor guilt is also common with PTSD, although seldom talked about on a first interview. The onset of workaholic tendencies can also be a clue to the diagnosis. The abrupt onset of substance abuse can also indicate the diagnosis of PTSD.

Courting danger is a symptom often specific for PTSD. Although people like mountain climbers and parachute jumpers take risks, the risks are calculated rather than impulsive. They work hard on planning to keep risks to a minimum. In contrast, PTSD patients often act on impulse, without adequate thought regarding consequences of their behavior.

REFERENCES

1. American Psychiatric Association: *Diagnostic and Statistical Manual of Mental Disorders, 3rd Edition, Revised.* Washington, DC, American Psychiatric Association.
2. Feinstein A: Posttraumatic stress disorder: a descriptive study supporting *DSM-III-R* criteria. *Am J Psychiatry 146:*665–666, 1989.
3. Solomon Z, Garb R, Bleich A, et al: Reactivation of combat-related post traumatic stress disorder. *Am J Psychiatry 144:*51–55, 1987a.
4. van der Kolk BA: *Psychological Trauma.* Washington, DC, American Psychiatric Press, 1986.
5. Scrignar CB: *Post Traumatic Stress Disorder.* Praeger Publishers, New York, 1984.
6. Pynoos RS, Frederick C, Nader K, Arroyo W, Steinberg A, Eth S, Nunez F, Fairbanks L: Life threat and posttraumatic stress in school-age children. *Arch Gen Psychiatry 44:*1057–1063, 1987.
7. Stretch RH, Figley CR: Combat and the Vietnam veteran: assessment of psychological adjustment. *Armed Forces and Society 10:*311–319, 1984.
8. McNally RJ, Lukach BM: Are panic attacks traumatic stressors? *Am J Psychiatry 149:*824–826, 1992.
9. Terri LC: Childhood traumas: an outline and overview. *Am J Psychiatry 148:*10–20, 1991.
10. van der Kolk B, Blitx R, Burr W, et al: Nightmares and trauma: a comparison of nightmares after combat with lifelong nightmares in veterans. *Am J Psychiatry 141:*187–190, 1984.
11. Kaminer H, Lavie P: Dreaming and long term adjustment to severe trauma. *Sleep Research 18:*146, 1988.
12. Blank AS Jr: The unconscious flashback to the war in Viet Nam veterans: clinical mystery, legal defense, and community problem, in *The Trauma of War: Stress and Recovery in Viet Nam Veterans.* Edited by Sonnenberg SM, Blank AS Jr, Talbott JA. Washington, DC, American Psychiatric Press, 1985, pp 293–308.
13. Behar D: Flashbacks and posttraumatic stress symptoms in combat veterans. *Compr Psychiatry 28:*459–466, 1987.
14. Mellman TA, Davis GC: Combat-related flashbacks in posttraumatic stress disorder: phenomenology and similarity to panic attacks. *J Clin Psychiatry 46:*379–382, 1985.
15. Geleerd ER, Hacker FJ, Rapaport D: Contributions to the study of amnesia and allied conditions. *Psychoanal Q 14:*199–220, 1945.

16. Loftus EF, Burns TE: Mental shock can produce retrograde amnesia. *Memory and Cognition 10:*318–323, 1982.

17. Sargent W, Slater E: Amnesic syndromes in war. *Proc R Soc Med 34:*757–764, 1941.

18. Christianson SA, Loftus EF: Remembering emotional events: the fate of detailed information. *Cognition and Emotion 5:*81–108, 1991.

19. Ross RJ, Ball W, Sullivan KA, et al: Sleep disturbance in posttraumatic stress disorder (letter). *Am J Psychiatry 147:*374, 1990.

20. van Kammen WB, Christiansen C, van Kammen DP, et al: Sleep and the POW experience: forty years later, in *Biological Assessment and Treatment of Post Traumatic Stress Disorder.* Edited by Giller EL. Washington, DC, American Psychiatric Press, 1990, pp 159–172.

21. Schlossberg A, Benjamin M: Sleep patterns in three acute combat fatigue cases. *J Clin Psychiatry 39:*546–549, 1978.

22. Yager J: Post combat violent behavior in psychiatrically maladjusting soldiers. *Arch Gen Psychiatry 33:*1332–1335, 1976.

23. Sutker PB, Winstead DK, Galina ZH, Allain AN: Cognitive deficits and psychopathology among former prisoners of war and combat veterans of the Korean conflict. *Am J Psychiatry 148:*67–72, 1991.

24. Keane TM, Gerardi RJ, Lyons JA, et al: The interrelationship of substance abuse and posttraumatic stress disorder: epidemiological and clinical considerations. *Recent Dev Alcohol 6:*27–48, 1988.

25. Kushner MG, Sher KJ, Beitman BD: The relation between alcohol problems and the anxiety disorders. *Am J Psychiatry 147:*685–695, 1990.

26. Branchey L, David W, Leiber CS: Alcoholism in Vietnam and Korea veterans: a long term follow-up. *Alcoholism: Clinical and Experimental Research 8:*572–575, 1984.

27. Southwick SM, Yehuda R, Giller EL Jr: Characterization of depression in war-related posttraumatic stress disorder. *Am J Psychiatry 148:*179–183, 1991.

28. Helzer JE, Robins LN, Davis DH: Depressive disorders in Vietnam returnees. *J Nerv Ment Dis 163:*177–185, 1976.

29. Sierles FS, Chen J-J, McFarland RE, Taylor MA: Posttraumatic stress disorder and concurrent psychiatric illness: a preliminary report. *Am J Psychiatry 140:*1177–1179, 1983.

30. Spiegel D, Cardena E: Dissociative mechanisms in posttraumatic stress disorder, in *Posttraumatic Stress Disorder: Etiology, Phenomenology and Treatment.* Edited by Wolf ME, Mosnaim AD. Washington, DC, American Psychiatric Press, 1990.

31. Bremner JD, Southwick S, Brett E, Fontana A, Rosenheck R, Charney DS: Dissociation and posttraumatic stress disorder in Vietnam combat veterans. *Am J Psychiatry 149:*328–332, 1992.

32. Cardeña E, Spiegel D: Dissociative reactions to the San Francisco Bay Area earthquake of 1989. *Am J Psychiatry 150:*474–478, 1993.

32. Riether AM, Stoudemire A: Psychogenic fugue state: a review. *South Med J 81:*568–571, 1988.

33. Ludwig AM: The psychobiological functions of dissociation. *Am J Clin Hypn* *26:*93–99, 1983.

34. Shatan CF: How do we turn off the guilt? *Human Behavior 2:*56–61, 1973.

35. Bremner JD, Scott TM, Delaney RC, et al: Deficits in short-term memory in posttraumatic stress disorder. *Am J Psychiatry 150:*1015–1019, 1993.

36. Pitman RK: Post-traumatic stress disorder, hormones, and memory. *Biol Psychiatry 26:*221–223, 1989.

37. Lipton MI, Schaffer WR: Post-traumatic stress disorder in the older veteran. *Milit Med 151:*522–524, 1986.

38. Pitman RK, Orr SP, Forgue DF, et al: Physiology of PTSD in Vietnam combat veterans. Paper presented at the 142nd annual meeting of the American Psychiatric Association, San Francisco, May 6–11, 1989.

39. Lipton MI, Schaffer WR: Physical symptoms related to post-traumatic stress disorder (PTSD) in an aging population. *Milit Med 153:*316–318, 1988.

40. Tapp WN, Levin BE, Natelson BH: Stress-induced heart failure. *Psychosom Med 45:*171–176, 1983.

41. Peters MN, Richardson CT: Stressful life events, acid hypersecretion, and ulcer disease. *Gastroenterology 84:*114–119, 1983.

42. Hendin H: Combat never ends: the paranoid adaptation to posttraumatic stress. *Am J Psychother 38:*121–131, 1984.

43. Domash MD, Sparr LF: Post-traumatic stress disorder masquerading as paranoid schizophrenia: a case report. *Milit Med 147:*772–774, 1982.

44. Davidson J, Swartz M, Storck M, Krishnan RR, Hammett EB: A diagnostic and family study of posttraumatic stress disorder. *Am J Psychiatry 142:*90–93, 1985.

45. Carol EM, Rueger DB, Foy DW, et al: Vietnam combat veterans with post traumatic stress disorder: analysis of marital and cohabitating adjustment. *J Abnorm Psychol 94:*329–337, 1985.

46. Green B, Grace M, Gleser G: Identifying survivors at risk, long-term impairment following the Beverly Hills Supper Club fire. *J Consult Clin Psychol 53:*672–678, 1985a.

47. Green B, Lindy J, Grace M, et al: Multiple diagnosis in posttraumatic stress disorder. *J Nerv Ment Dis 177:*329–335, 1989.

SECTION III
PREVENTION

This section is comprised of a single chapter, aptly titled *Prevention of PTSD*. The various aspects of primary, secondary, and tertiary prevention are reviewed in detail. Many helpful suggestions and recommendations are made.

Chapter 40

PREVENTION OF PTSD

GENERAL

In recent years we have come to better understand that everyone has feelings and gets upset after experiencing trauma, and that everyone has a breaking point. It is common for the effects of trauma to last for years, even for a lifetime.[1] Everyone has heard an example of some person who suffered trauma in childhood that affected them throughout life. However, not everyone who is traumatized suffers long term symptoms and disability. Some people don't get as upset by a traumatic experience because they have somehow learned ways beforehand to deal with it more effectively. Others are able to get over it gradually, with or without help. If the effects of trauma are to be kept to a minimum, therefore, it is important for us to learn how to prevent or minimize strong reactions to traumatic events, and should they occur, how to keep them to a minimum in both intensity and duration.

BEFOREHAND PREPARATION FOR DEALING WITH TRAUMA (PRIMARY PREVENTION)

By definition, *primary prevention*[2] involves efforts to reduce or eliminate factors that cause or contribute to the development of illness. Many potentially traumatic events are predictable. It therefore makes sense to teach people to deal with such events beforehand so they are not caught by surprise. When they are fully prepared for what happens, they know what to expect, what to do, how to handle the situation, and can do so with a minimum of anxiety and upsetting after effects.[3] We are familiar with examples like first aid training, and fire drills and disaster drills in schools, businesses, and industry. Various training programs include the teaching of people to better handle emergencies. Examples include the military, police, firefighters, emergency personnel, medical personnel, paramedics, and industrial employees like those who work in munitions or atomic energy plants.

Most of these training programs for dealing with emergencies are comprehensive, but tend to leave out the human factor. That can result in people involved in a disaster knowing what to do mechanically, but unprepared to deal with their own overwhelming feelings and emotions. In my own experience, for example, I already described my overwhelming and embarrassing fear on entering combat, for which I was completely unprepared despite extensive training. Talking to anyone about my fear was unthinkable. Likewise, in my medical training afterwards, I don't recall any discussion of personal feelings when dealing with traumatized patients who may be seriously injured or disfigured, bleeding and screaming in pain. Emergency medical personnel are therefore often troubled by symptoms of PTSD.

Specific education, training and conditioning are therefore necessary prior to a disaster or traumatic situation. Every individual must gain competence and confidence in using equipment and in dealing with all possible contingencies. Confidence is boosted further by the knowledge that they have the finest equipment. For those working in an atomic energy plant, for example, an understanding of the total operation is important, along with thorough knowledge and competence in what each person must do, plus assignments and procedures in dealing with various possible contingencies and emergencies. In a military combat unit, each individual must learn the use of various weapons, learn all appropriate procedures and tactics, how to deal with all possible contingencies, and achieve a personal level of physical fitness necessary for the rigors of the military mission. These two examples serve to illustrate the fact that people who feel competent to handle their equipment and to deal with any given situation are under less stress during an emergency or trauma. They are therefore less vulnerable to PTSD. Confidence in the quality of equipment confers additional reassurance.

Confidence in leadership is also important in reducing the level of stress. This confidence includes the conviction that top leadership people have integrity, fully support the organization and each individual, and can be depended upon for accurate information, for obtaining the best equipment, providing the best training, and hiring top people up and down the line. Those in leadership positions at all levels must demonstrate their knowledge, ability, dependability, and full support of all those under them without showing favoritism. Good leadership makes for a confident and efficient organization.

Confidence in one's comrades and fellow employees that develops during training is also essential to keep the level of stress low. Each individual must know what others can do, and that they can be depended upon whatever happens. An organization that does all these things well has high esprit de corps and a good feeling of camaraderie.

Additionally, training should include opportunities for discussion of feelings and emotions. Everyone in a police or military unit, for example, must understand and talk about the fact that at times they will be terribly frightened, that it is normal to feel frightened in the face of danger, and that everybody gets frightened. However, they must also learn that even though frightened, their training will enable them to do what is needed, and at such times they can depend on their leaders and comrades for full support. Since people in an organization must depend on one another to deal with the emergency or traumatic situation, learning to maintain good communication in those emergency times and afterwards is essential. People can help one another get through the ordeal by communicating not only about what is going on, but also about their feelings, stress level, state of fatigue, etc. Doing so reduces stress and enhances the feelings of control.

Primary Prevention in a school could build from the customary fire drills that teach students how to behave during a fire. Students should also have some first aid training so they would know how to help themselves and others who may be injured in a fire, or in any type of disaster. A shooting in school is another type of disaster. Such knowledge and training would serve to reduce anxiety if disaster strikes, and therefore reduce the possibility of anyone developing PTSD.[4] In addition, school discussions should be held periodically to remind students that fear is natural in an emergency, nothing to be ashamed of, and that training enables one to do the appropriate things despite fear. For example, some discussion of their feelings while trying to help someone in pain would be helpful.

On a personal level, similar primary prevention is appropriate. Everyone should know what to do if they fall, are in an auto or bicycle accident, if they are threatened or assaulted, or meet any other emergency. For example, everyone should know that if they are trapped in a car following an accident, they must try to remain as calm as possible during efforts to remove them. Using this example, most people have never thought about this happening to them, or about how they would feel. They are therefore more vulnerable to being caught by surprise, and then react in panic if it happens. Reducing the frequency and severity of such reactions is a highly desirable goal.

SECONDARY PREVENTION FOLLOWING TRAUMA

General

Secondary prevention[5] includes early detection and implementation of treatment at the earliest possible time. Secondary prevention for PTSD during the trauma and soon thereafter has a number of components.

Limiting Exposure, Rest

Stress reactions and PTSD can be prevented or kept to a minimum by limiting exposure. For example, firefighters dealing with a dangerous fire are exposed to possible injury and death while performing physically strenuous tasks in high or low temperatures. They can be relieved at set time intervals for rest, relaxation, hot food, and associating with pleasant, understanding people while doing so. Knowing that your exposure to danger is time limited seems to make a big difference in your ability to tolerate stress. The opportunity to get away and relax and rest, even though temporary, is restorative and rejuvenating. Recognizing that limitation of exposure helps morale, tours of duty during the war in Vietnam were limited to one year. Even during that one year, opportunities for rest were provided periodically whenever possible. Such things were done to some extent in previous wars. However, war conditions can prohibit rests of any kind.

In my personal war experience, I recall a strong yearning for a break in the constant daily pressure and stress. Just a few days to relax, sleep safely and eat some good meals would have done wonders. I'm sure I could have returned to the fray refreshed and better able to deal with the stress. Knowing that no such respite was forthcoming made it weigh more heavily, and it was more difficult to bear. Some soldiers in combat talk about "the million dollar wound," meaning an injury that is not too serious, but serious enough to give you a rest in a hospital. This is a good example of the importance of rest and respite. Whatever the stressful or dangerous situation or event, limiting periods of exposure helps morale and ability to tolerate even the worst stress. When the individual knows that relief will come at a set time, ability to tolerate trauma and stress improves. It is desirable to include regular breaks during the emergency as part of training for dealing with disaster so that everyone knows how long they must endure before obtaining relief and rest once training ends and the real stress begins.

Debriefing (The First Step in Controlling the Effects of Trauma)

Most people are familiar with this term from the military, where individuals, or groups of individuals, talk about what happened upon returning from a mission. We also hear reports of astronauts going through debriefing after returning to earth.

When someone suffers a traumatic experience, the first step in controlling after effects and preventing the development of PTSD should be debriefing. For debriefing to be most effective, it should be done as soon as possible after the trauma, the sooner the better. During debriefing the individual should have full opportunity to talk about what happened to a sympathetic and understanding listener. The listener should be very familiar with the specific trauma, and if possible should be someone who has gone through similar trauma. When listeners have had similar experience, there is more confidence in their ability to fully understand. In addition to reviewing specific facts about the traumatic event, it is important to include the feelings and emotions involved. If the expected fear was felt, it is best talked about.

When a group of people has suffered trauma, they should be together during debriefing. It is important that each individual hear how others suffered the same traumatic experiences, and hear that others react with feelings and emotions similar to theirs. This helps avoid the usual isolation and stigma felt by all participants who are convinced that their pain and suffering is different and worse than anyone else. The group debriefing fosters group cohesion, group discussion, and reassuring dialogue between individuals in the group. This prepares people for the next step, which is group discussion (group therapy).

In the military, debriefing has often not included all the above desirable aspects. During World War II, for example, B17 crews had a debriefing on return from every mission. The debriefer for each bomber crew was from intelligence, interested only in what each individual saw, how many planes of what type, etc. Since that person had never flown, he was not considered capable of fully understanding what went on in the air.

Feelings were naturally never talked about. However, I think that the opportunity for each individual to feel verified by hearing crewmates talking about what happened was very therapeutic and helpful even though the debriefing was so limited.

In my own experience with military training, if the possibility of fear was ever mentioned, I never seriously considered that it could happen to me. I apparently preferred to not even think about it. Therefore, when our first two days of combat were particularly severe, my feelings went beyond fear. Sheer terror would be a more accurate description. As already described, such feelings took me completely by surprise (John Wayne never became nervous under fire). It would have been much different if there were serious talks and discussions about this during training, plus debriefing opportunities after those first two days of combat. In saying this, I realize that debriefing in military combat may be impossible for periods of time, but it would help even when done later.

After a fire or other disaster in a factory, business, or school, prompt debriefing by experienced therapists is essential, followed by other secondary prevention measures that are described here.

Individual, Group, and Family Therapy

After a group of people experience a trauma and have had at least one debriefing session, smaller groups of ten to twelve people should be formed. Each group should be led by a professional who is trained in group therapy who should also be a sympathetic, understanding listener, and if possible, someone who has been through a similar traumatic experience. That is because of the common conviction that, "Nobody can really understand what we went through unless they have been through it themselves." Everyone has some of these feelings.

In reviewing preparation prior to trauma or disaster, one suggestion I made was that the large organization or large units be broken into small discussion groups. Following trauma and debriefing, the same small group should stay together since they already relate to one another and to the issues. When group assignments have not been made in advance, individuals must be assigned to groups. An individual who was traumatized while alone, such as a rape victim or single vehicle accident victim, should be placed (after debriefing) into a small group of people who experienced similar trauma.

The overwhelming horror of many traumatic experiences takes people by surprise, even when there has been prior planning, rehearsal, and discussion. The preparation helps reduce, but does not eliminate serious emotional upsets and the possibility of developing PTSD.

Following a disaster, group discussions should occur daily, if necessary, and reduced to weekly as soon as everyone is comfortable with doing so. In most instances, those who benefit from group sessions will gradually feel less need for such help after a variable number of weeks. The sessions can be terminated when everyone involved feels comfortable that they are no longer needed. At that time, it is highly unlikely that any participants will develop symptoms of PTSD in the future, which is the goal of all this effort.

Individual therapy, in addition to group therapy, is often indicated for the following reasons. Some people have difficulty entering a group and may also need help in learning to take problems to the group. Concerns about group can be discussed in individual therapy. People are also helped in individual sessions to understand that their symptoms and concerns are not different from the others, and that group discussion is the best source of help for part of these problems. When the individual becomes comfortable as a group member, individual visits usually become less necessary. However, an individual visit may still be requested at times for help with special problems or concerns.

Since a traumatic event affects everyone in a family or organization, appropriate help must be directed to everyone involved. Family meetings should therefore be held for immediate family members of disaster victims. At such meetings, problems and symptoms can be explained, and family members have the opportunity to ask questions and receive answers. If the trauma involved a large group of men on a construction project, for example, their wives and children would be included in family meetings and then in family therapy. If the trauma involved one section of a plant or factory, all workers in the plant or factory should be included in meetings and therapeutic discussion groups. These meetings should last only as long as they are needed.

Therefore, if those who are traumatized have had appropriate beforehand preparation, debriefing immediately after the trauma, followed by a period of individual, group, and family therapy, the incidence of long term PTSD symptoms and disability should be greatly reduced or eliminated.

Coping with Ongoing Trauma

Some professions and types of work or activity expose individuals, or groups of individuals, to trauma repeatedly, and sometimes frequently. Examples include emergency medical personnel, police, firefighters, and military combat personnel. Emergency medical personnel are traumatized repeatedly by dealing with death, severely injured and bleeding patients who may cry or scream in pain, and by disturbed relatives or bystanders. No matter how terrible the situation, they are required to be cool, calm, and professional. Included are paramedics, staff members that work in emergency rooms or centers, burn centers, and other medical staff that responds to disasters and emergencies. These people need preparation before starting this line of work, debriefing immediately after particularly traumatic experiences, and regular ongoing group meetings in which they can talk comfortably with one another about experiences and emotional reactions and give one another support. Well run programs should greatly reduce or eliminate PTSD in those groups that are at high risk for developing PTSD.

As previously indicated, the macho code and need to maintain the image of being tough, keeps most people from admitting to feelings and emotions in response to trauma. This is particularly true for police, firefighters, military, and others who have traditionally avoided the issue of emotions and disability caused by PTSD. The police officer who gets shot is not only traumatized emotionally, but in addition views injury as a sign of failure, of having blundered. It is never talked about. All police and fire units should have beforehand preparation, as described, that includes discussion groups. These discussion groups or units must meet regularly to discuss issues and feelings. If a police officer or firefighter is injured on duty, debriefing and regular group meetings remain essential if long term PTSD and disability is to be avoided. Some such programs have already been started but most departments need help in order to start dealing with these serious problems.

The same is true for the military, who also need the beforehand preparation, continuation of regular group or unit discussions, and debriefing after particularly traumatic incidents. During military combat, regularly scheduled group or unit meetings may not be possible. However, they should take place whenever conditions permit. When you can't do all the ideal things, you do as much as possible.

TERTIARY PREVENTION

By definition, tertiary prevention is aimed at the reduction or elimination of residual disability after illness. With PTSD, therefore, tertiary prevention is aimed at the symptoms and disability associated with chronic and long-term PTSD. It therefore includes dealing with the many symptoms of the disorder. Since most of this book is written about these symptoms and their treatment, they will not be enumerated here.

REFERENCES

1. Helzer JE, Robins LN, McEvoy L: Posttraumatic stress disorder in the general population. *N Engl J Med 317:*1630–1634, 1987.
2. Williams C, Solomon SD, Bartone P: Primary prevention in aircraft disasters: integrating research and theory. *Am Psychol 43:*730–739, 1988.
3. Pynoos RS, Frederick C, Nader K, et al: Life threat and posttraumatic stress in school-age children. *Arch Gen Psychiatry 44:*1057–1063, 1987.
4. Nader K, Pynoos R, Fairbanks L, et al: Children's PTSD reactions one year after a sniper attack on their school. *Am J Psychiatry 147:*1526–1530, 1990.
5. Stokes J: Management of combat stress and battle fatigue: current information on US Army Medical Department doctrine. Fort Sam Houston, Texas, US Army Academy of Health Sciences, Nov 5, 1990.

SECTION IV
TREATMENT

This section begins with chapters on considerations in planning treatment, goals of treatment, modalities of treatment, helpful suggestions for treatment, and treatment of acute symptoms.

As in Section II, the treatment of each symptom is then described in a separate chapter. This includes each symptom listed in *DSM-III-R,* and the nineteen additional symptoms.

The final two chapters are on medication and on duration of treatment.

Chapter 41

CONSIDERATIONS IN PLANNING TREATMENT

The planning of a comprehensive PTSD program must include both prevention beforehand as well as treatment after the trauma or disaster. Questions that must be addressed in planning include what you are going to do and why, and how to coordinate efforts to meet the various objectives. As already indicated, I believe that this is best accomplished by keeping things simple and uncomplicated, and using a common sense approach.

My personal approach to treatment has been strongly influenced by painful personal experience with PTSD, as well as treating the problem since 1981. I feel that two powerful factors must be dealt with constantly in all efforts toward prevention and treatment. These two factors are *loss of control* and *stigma*.

LOSS OF CONTROL

Loss of control is always very frightening, and there are various ways in which one can lose control. My own loss of control associated with PTSD involved ruminations, or the reexperiencing of traumatic war events. I lived in dread of it starting because I had no way to predict it, and no way to prevent it from starting (no control). Once it started, I suffered the consequences, and felt completely helpless to reduce either the severity or duration of suffering. I simply had to hope it would end soon. In a sense, it took over, and I had absolutely no control. The helplessness and inability to control is a terrible and frightening experience that I can still remember very clearly even though it has been many years. My life was literally run by this fear. I thought about it constantly in anticipation and dread. It became the overwhelming and most important part of day to day living.

Feeling helpless and unable to exert any control in this manner is an experience familiar to those with emotional disorders including PTSD, anxiety, panic, and depression. One feels overwhelmed, and helpless to

105

resist it starting, or to control intensity or duration once it strikes. Living in such fear and anticipation produces terrible suffering. It runs your life. In addition, when you have PTSD, this constant stress triggers additional ruminations and the reliving of traumatic episodes, which further aggravates all the other problems.

I therefore feel strongly that dealing with helplessness and loss of control must be a priority from the very beginning of treatment. Motivation for treatment is maintained by the strong need to regain and maintain control.

Starting with the first treatment visit, I do two things to bolster feelings of control. One is to explain PTSD, the various symptoms, and how it all works. Knowing what to expect and how things work reduces the helplessness of constantly being taken by surprise. In addition, this knowledge is used with the second aspect of control, the learning of specific strategies. Learning what to do to prevent a problem from starting, or if it starts, what will help, is a way of having tools to work with. The individual with tools is no longer helpless. Something can be done for each particular problem. The regaining of control and diminishing helplessness is an important theme throughout treatment. This should be appreciated when reading all parts of the treatment section. In addition, the description of each symptom and how it works provides information that can be used to improve control.

STIGMA

Feelings of stigma are more important than most people appreciate. In dealing with PTSD, we have already considered my personal example of combat experience. Convinced that I was the only one with such fear, beginning the first day of combat, I felt there was something wrong with me. This was a feeling of being defective, abnormal, and less than a man. I was painfully aware of feeling defective and not as good as others throughout the combat experience and afterwards. I would never consider talking to anyone about these deeply held and shameful feelings. Exposing my shame was unthinkable. My self-esteem remained very low, I felt inferior to everyone else, and always tried to hide it. Powerful feelings of this nature are part of the reason why those suffering from PTSD avoid talking about the problem, and even deny symptoms when asked specifically about them. The terrible secret cannot be revealed, whatever the cost.

A related aspect of stigma is the cultural bias regarding any problem that can be classified as mental illness. If one has a problem requiring the help of a mental health professional, they tend to be thought of as "crazy" and automatically not as good as a "normal" person. People avoid seeing a psychiatrist for help with a problem because of concern that they would be disgraced, laughed at, and looked down upon by friends and family. In addition, the fact that they have seen a psychiatrist at some time could cause loss of a job or license. These are the harsh realities of our society that reinforce low feelings of self-worth and self-esteem in those suffering from PTSD, and make it harder to talk about.

Feelings of stigma must therefore be addressed in treatment. If it were not addressed, patients would be less able to discuss their feelings and symptoms, which is a necessary part of treatment and the healing process.

Most important from the beginning of treatment is to keep the facts clear that PTSD is *normal*, that it can happen to anyone who "has experienced an event that is outside the range of usual human experience and that would be markedly distressing to almost anyone." This quote from the official book of diagnosis indicates that anyone can suffer symptoms of PTSD, that everyone has a breaking point. Having strong emotions in response to trauma is normal, so PTSD is therefore normal, not abnormal, and feelings of stigma and inferiority are unwarranted. If you are frightened by a trauma that threatens death or serious injury, such fear means you are normal. You would not be considered normal if you were not frightened and upset by such a threat or trauma. For example, if the enemy in military combat is trying to kill you, fear is expected. If you were not frightened under these circumstances, you wouldn't be normal. Expecting yourself to not be frightened is unreasonable and unrealistic. Patients must learn to adjust their attitudes to these facts. It usually requires a reversal of the way they have felt about these issues. The reader should recognize that stigma is also addressed throughout by the explanation of PTSD, description of associated symptoms, and the logical steps in treatment.

ADDITIONAL CONSIDERATIONS

An additional consideration in approaching treatment for PTSD relates to the unique symptoms of ruminations. When a trauma is reexperienced, it is with the full emotional intensity of the original experience. Time does not diminish the powerful emotions, as we have come to expect with most unpleasant and upsetting life experiences.

Most people expect a problem to be helped only by going back and talking about the past experience in detail (repeatedly if necessary) in order to arrive at a better understanding and peace of mind. I consider PTSD an exception to the usual treatment approach because going back to the past merely triggers ruminations and increased emotional trauma and suffering. Learning to leave the past behind and stop spending time with it appears to be a more successful approach to treatment, allowing one to go on with life.

This must be explained to patients when they start treatment. Many of those I have treated had difficulty with this concept. There is often the feeling that it is not treatment unless you go back and talk about the past. Once people understand the reason for a different approach, they recognize the validity of this reasoning. I am then apt to hear from those who were in other PTSD programs that talking about the trauma in every treatment session was very upsetting.

Chapter 42

GOALS OF TREATMENT

Treatment must be directed at accomplishing definite goals. Goals must therefore be considered before treatment begins. Some goals must be attained, at least in part, before work on other goals can begin. Since individualized treatment is best, the specific goals of each individual must be addressed.

An important goal of treatment is the relief of specific symptoms. The list of PTSD symptoms is long, and many patients have had their lives disrupted by these symptoms. Substance abuse, for example, is a common symptom that causes serious life problems. Control of substance abuse is therefore one important goal of treatment. Ruminations have been described as central to all other symptoms, and patients must learn to reduce time spent reliving traumatic events in order to get well. In addition, when someone spends a large part of their day reliving past events, the time is stolen from today and tomorrow. The past cannot be changed, only the future. I often say to patients that an important goal of treatment is to learn to leave the past behind, to stop spending so much time with the past because it robs you of the present and future. Anger and temper are frequently troublesome symptoms, and learning to control temper is essential. The treatment of each symptom on the list will be reviewed.

Medical and physical symptoms must likewise be treated, since physical and emotional health go hand in hand. Physical pain, or concern about medical conditions, can interfere with treatment. Medical and physical problems are commonly associated with PTSD, as already discussed. The psychiatrist must therefore work closely with other medical specialists toward the goal of restoring the health of all patients.

Another goal of treatment is restoration of family functioning. Comprehensive treatment therefore includes family therapy, marital therapy, or both if indicated. Once family functioning has improved, all family members feel more secure to move from the family circle to interact with the broad community and take on the challenges of returning to employment.[1]

Restoration of job functioning is therefore another goal of treatment. The patient can move toward employment when specific symptoms are adequately relieved, physical and medical problems have been dealt with, and family functioning provides a solid home base. Restored ability to maintain gainful employment gives a big boost to pride and self esteem.

A specific example of setting goals would be a PTSD patient who is alcoholic, distressed by symptoms much of the time, who has not worked for two years. His wife is threatening to leave. The first goal is control of alcohol use. While that is worked on, the goal of relieving symptoms must begin and physical health must be restored. Also work must begin as soon as possible on the goal of restored family functioning, and finally, the goal of return to gainful employment.

Chapter 43

MODALITIES OF TREATMENT

GENERAL

Modalities of treatment include group therapy, individual therapy, family therapy, marital therapy, day treatment program, and inpatient hospital treatment. The various modalities must be combined in the most therapeutic way and must be consistent. What happens in one area of therapy must relate to what is happening in other aspects of treatment, so all efforts are combined and mutually supportive. Good treatment requires good communication between the various therapists. Time for staff meetings is therefore vital, since therapists must be saying similar things to the patient and combining their efforts most effectively. When therapists contradict one another, even inadvertently, patients become confused, and treatment is impaired. In addition, the treatment program for each patient should be individualized, even when patients have similar trauma and similar problems. The various treatment modalities must be parts of a comprehensive treatment program tailored to the needs of each individual.

GROUP THERAPY

Group therapy is usually considered to be the most effective modality of treatment for PTSD.[2] This appears to be true for a number of reasons. Learning that other group members have similar feelings and symptoms is always therapeutic, since PTSD patients usually feel different from others and think they are more seriously disturbed than anyone else. In addition, group members are peers who feel comfortable and secure that others in the group fully understand the problems and feelings under discussion since they have had similar experiences and problems. For many, group becomes the place they are most comfortable, and may be the only place they can relax in the presence of other people. Peers always have special communication between one another, and this understanding is best utilized to support therapeutic goals. It requires a good relationship between patients and staff, avoiding some common problems in treatment like an "us against them" feeling toward staff on the part of group members.

One troublesome problem in treatment is the tendency for patients to come in with the covert attitude of, "Here I am. Cure me, I dare you." This attitude can result in patients and staff being adversarial rather than being mutually supportive. Keeping these problems to a minimum requires the staff to respect all patients, and to respect their experience and understanding of symptoms and problems. When staff members feel they have all the knowledge and all the answers, patients in the group resent it. A group of patients taught me this early in my career when I still thought I had all the answers. Every time I gave the answer to a problem in that group, someone would say, "Well, doc, maybe you read that in a book somewhere, but you were never in that situation like we were." Such rejection of my "good answers" was most frustrating until I got the message that their experience gave them a legitimate role in finding answers.

Since then I have felt strongly that the most effective group leader does not provide answers but helps group members work out answers on the basis of their personal knowledge and experience. When a group member says, "When I had that problem, doing such and such helped," other group members strongly respect the validity of the statement. At such times, the good therapist will give positive feedback to the individual who is trying to help friends by virtue of personal trial and experience. The therapist is most effective when raising questions needing answers from the group, rather than trying to give answers. Answers and suggestions are always better accepted from peers than from staff. This represents a change of role for therapists who are in the habit of providing answers or guidance in finding answers. At best, I feel that the therapist provides guidance about group process.

This describes group therapy in which group members carry major responsibility for the success of treatment. The responsibility is reinforced by the fact that *you get your best help in the process of helping others.* Group members feel responsible to help when anyone presents a problem. They help by giving opinions and sharing personal experience with the particular problem. The one getting help can hear about more than one way of dealing with the problem, and can develop an answer that is individually most fitting. Group members functioning in this manner are true peers in terms of the problems. Issues of status are therefore kept to a minimum. In a veteran group, for example, group members are all equals whether they were privates or officers of high rank. Group work is therefore not distracted by such irrelevant issues. With a group atmosphere of everyone working together with mutual respect (including staff), transference problems are kept to a minimum.

I am often amazed at the intensity and insight achieved in some group meetings despite lack of technical input by staff. Staff responsibilities in group include calling attention (for group consideration) to departures from the topic under discussion or departures from attitudes that are most constructive. Staff must be seen as group advocates interested in helping everyone (without preference), and interested in group decisions, rather than providing answers, telling people what to do, or admonishing. I often say that I am more like a teacher than anything else. I can describe a problem or symptom, and how it works. With this knowledge, group members can proceed to make decisions on the basis of objective information. Staff members recognize the authority of group decisions, so changes in schedule or policy are approved by consensus.

In this group atmosphere, arguments and fights between group members are virtually unknown. Angry, aggressive, or hostile individuals are always much better controlled by a responsible group than by an authoritarian staff member. Hostility of one group member toward another has been a very rare exception over the years in PTSD groups with which I have been involved. This is particularly noteworthy because many group members suffering from PTSD have serious problems with anger, temper, and self-control. History of temper problems are therefore rarely a concern with referral to PTSD group unless the individual is also sociopathic. In general, a group that has genuine responsibility for treatment controls irresponsible behavior of an individual better than authoritarian staff.

Group therapy is best held weekly, since longer gaps between meetings tend to cause a loss of continuity. Meetings should last either sixty or ninety minutes. The longer time gives the advantage of completing a good discussion. When there is a choice, I favor the ninety minute group therapy format.

A group session best begins with inquiries as to whether anyone in the group has a problem they would like to bring up for discussion. It is best that a discussion be started by a group member rather than staff. If a staff member suggests a subject too quickly, it can cut off the individual who needs a little time before bringing up something that is difficult to talk about. When staff suggests the subject, the group may comply but can resent authoritarian pressure. This gets into some of the non-productive games that must be avoided if therapy is to be most helpful and productive. Staff should always be viewed as helping and encouraging a democratic group process and group responsibility for finding answers. For example, if a staff member indicates that the group has strayed from the problem under discussion, it should never be viewed as an admonition. Rather, the staff member should be perceived as trying to help the group find answers to the problem at hand, since straying defeats what the group wants to do. What the group wants or needs always comes first, rather than what a staff member wants.

Since group discussion can easily provide triggers for ruminations, frequent discussions of trauma can be upsetting and is best avoided. The group therefore functions best when members are helping one another to reduce triggers and ruminations, to control temper, and improve social relationships. However, there are often problems from the past trauma that continue to trouble individuals. This is referred to as *unfinished business.* When a group member's problem becomes too troublesome, the group will review that person's trauma. Other group members make suggestions to help the individual leave the past problems behind and not continue to spend time with them, which is an important goal of therapy. They may reassure the individual that a correct decision was made or give supportive and objective feedback on the trauma. These opinions are always respected and appreciated.

A discussion like this can be upsetting for all group members, since triggers for their own traumatic memories may be touched. Many group members can remain more upset than usual for several days afterwards. However, all participants understand that when someone else's problem is discussed and helped, part of their own problem is also helped. Group members come to recognize that even though some meetings can be difficult and upsetting, they are getting help in the process. Staff members can make the suggestion of limiting the time spent with trauma when they feel that continuing the discussion would be counterproductive.

At times it is natural for a group of people with similar trauma to start exchanging memories about the trauma. In veteran PTSD groups this is referred to as *telling war stories.* If a group member does not point this out to the others fairly soon, it is a staff responsibility to ask about what is going on. This is usually sufficient to remind everyone they are doing something that is not in their best interest, since they know that such triggers are best avoided.

Early in treatment, regular group attendance should be encouraged (but not demanded) in order to help the individual as quickly as possible. Each person must be aware of their responsibilities in the recovery process. Once someone is feeling better and getting into more activities with family and friends, they may miss meetings because of a trip or event. This can be seen as positive, since we like to see improvement and increased outside activity and independence. Individual therapy may be reduced or terminated, although individual visits are arranged whenever a patient requests one.

Many patients entering a PTSD group have been socially withdrawn for some time, and the group can be the only place in which an individual is comfortable with other people. Therefore, one of the first steps in returning to social activity can be group members meeting on the outside. Two or more group members can decide to meet and go to a movie, restaurant, bowling, fishing, etc. Such activities are always encouraged.

A summary of the advantages of this innovative approach to group therapy starts with staff attitudes that foster responsible therapeutic effort more consistently, and keeps games and transference problems to a minimum. The "here I am, cure me" problem is avoided by a group atmosphere in which peers expect responsible behavior from one another so they can all get maximum benefit. Aggressive behavior is therefore well controlled. Self-esteem of group members is enhanced by staff respect for their experience and opinions, for their ability to provide answers, as well as by pride in helping others (since most help comes from other group members rather than staff). Group members come to feel relatively comfortable in revealing their problems and secrets. Staff responsibility includes providing the atmosphere in which all this can take place.

INDIVIDUAL THERAPY

All patients coming into a PTSD treatment program are initially evaluated by an individual therapist for diagnosis and motivation for treatment. When hospitalization is unnecessary and treatment is indicated, outpatient treatment is explained, and symptoms are discussed and reviewed. The patient is scheduled for weekly individual therapy lasting one hour to maintain continuity of treatment. If a longer period elapses, many things previously discussed must be repeated. The patient is also referred to group for weekly group therapy whenever this option is available. When group therapy is not available, individual therapy alone can still be very helpful and is recommended.

During weekly individual therapy, relevant symptoms and problems are discussed. One of the first problems often discussed is the patient's reluctance to join the group. Facing any group of people is usually difficult for PTSD patients, no less a group in which one is expected to reveal sensitive problems and information. Most individuals need reassurance and explanation before attempting to join the group. They are reminded that others in the group have symptoms and problems similar to theirs. They are also told that they are not obliged to talk in group, and can just sit and listen the first few times. I often urge patients to try attending group just once or twice before making a final decision not to do so. Once they have sat in the group, they usually feel comfortable in a short time and are willing to continue group participation.

Many times individuals tell me about a troublesome problem. Rather than suggesting a solution, I often advise them that they can get the best help for that problem in the group. When they say they could never talk about it in group, I offer to help them do so. I also tell them that while the secret is between the two of us, it is still a deep dark secret that continues to bother them. Once they have talked about it in group, the secret is out in the open, the expected criticism does not occur, and the problem is no longer as troublesome as before. With this type of explanation and encouragement, most patients will finally agree to bring the problem up in group if I offer to help. The group can be depended upon to respond in a sensitive, positive and understanding way. During discussion, others in the group will often admit that they have, or have had, a similar problem.

Individual therapy is often helpful in reminding and reinforcing helpful suggestions learned in group. Individual and group therapy reinforce one another in helping the individual learn to deal with problems more effectively. When the patient is having a difficult time coping with problems, I usually continue weekly individual therapy in addition to the group therapy. Only when the patient becomes comfortable in doing so do we phase out individual visits and continue with only group therapy. However, individual therapy or consultation is always provided whenever the patient feels the need, and that usually occurs when a special problem arises. Here again, with a special problem I often advise people to take the problem to the group.

During individual therapy, the therapist's attitude and approach is similar to group therapy. The therapist is more of a teacher, explaining how things work, is always clearly on the patient's side as a strong advocate for the patient without telling the patient what to do. Transference problems are therefore kept to a minimum.

Individual therapy is often a time that specific family problems are discussed. Since patients with PTSD usually have many family problems, the benefits of family and marital therapy can be discussed. Such therapy can be in addition to or in place of the individual visits.

Finally, medical problems and medication issues can be discussed during individual therapy. Appropriate referrals are made to medical specialists, the benefits of medication are discussed, questions about side effects are answered, and changes in medication or in dose of medication can be arranged.

MARITAL AND FAMILY THERAPY

When someone experiences trauma, their emotions and behavior are usually affected. These changes impact the entire family. When the initial reaction proceeds to full-blown PTSD, the family needs help over a longer period of time.

Families must be involved after trauma so they can be helped to understand and deal with changes in the patient. They must avoid getting angry at symptoms they don't understand. An understanding family can help the patient overcome problems more rapidly so that the entire family unit can get back to normal functioning as soon as possible. Questions of family members must be answered regarding symptoms, and they must learn how they can help the patient. This can help the family unit learn to communicate and deal with problems more effectively, yielding long lasting and positive results.

When the patient develops PTSD, the various symptoms must be understood by all family members. The patient could have symptoms like staying alone in the bedroom for long periods, preoccupied much of the time, unable to sleep or keep a schedule, reluctant to leave the house, and have a frightening temper. Children can be helped to understand the symptoms and what they can do to help. Interactions and communication with the patient can be improved by such efforts.

Usually the heaviest burden falls on the spouse, who finds it difficult to understand and cope with the many changes. For example, a formerly gentle and loving husband can become distant, avoid close contact, and could accuse his wife of infidelity or stealing his money. He could also have a nasty temper that causes her to fear for her safety, and he may be unable to work and earn a living. Marital therapy is necessary to help husband and wife reestablish communication and learn to work together on the various problems in order to improve the marital relationship.

An example of a problem dealt with in marital therapy is ruminations. Both husband and wife come to understand the importance of reducing the time spent reliving traumatic experiences. Although the patient is often unaware of drifting into this, the spouse can quickly observe what is happening and inform the patient. The patient can then work on ending the rumination quickly. One problem in doing so is that when told about this, the patient often gets angry at the spouse. These angry responses must be worked on in marital therapy if the spouse is to continue to give this type of help.

Since impotence and loss of interest in sex are often symptoms of PTSD, such problems are also addressed in marital therapy. A spouse must learn that such changes do not represent loss of love, and that the symptoms can gradually improve with encouragement and sympathetic understanding.

A spouse can also learn not to take anger and temper personally, but to understand where it comes from. Since temper problems are common with PTSD, they are often discussed during marital therapy.

During my years of working with veterans suffering from PTSD, I was always impressed by the many wives who stayed with and helped their husbands over a number of years despite his bad temper, loss of interest in sex, and many other symptoms. The wives were always anxious to learn about and understand symptoms and behaviors of their husbands that were perplexing, worrisome, and often frightening. For example, behavior during nightmares was often a problem. A wife must understand why her husband starts jerking, moaning or screaming during the night, or gets up to do things he doesn't remember in the morning. She should also get information on what to do when he starts into a nightmare so she can awaken him fully to safely end the nightmare.

SPOUSE GROUPS

As already discussed, spouses of those suffering from PTSD are often faced with many difficult, upsetting, and frustrating problems. These problems can be difficult to deal with even with the help of family and marital therapy. It is therefore logical to offer the spouses additional help with group therapy.

My only experience of this nature was in the Veterans Administration Medical Center. Group therapy was offered to the wives of veterans who were in treatment for PTSD. The wives had the opportunity in group to compare notes on specific problems, to discuss the problems, and to hear the experience of those who had found ways to understand and cope with the problems. Many wives found it to be quite helpful.

These groups of wives were usually popular for several weeks but never lasted much longer than that. Interest waned, and fewer and fewer attended meetings. When that happened, future meetings were canceled.

Such groups were helpful to those who participated. I think that spouse groups could be appropriate and helpful in other PTSD programs, whatever the type of trauma involved. This type of group will usually be short term, if my previous experience is any indication.

PARTIAL HOSPITALIZATION

Partial hospitalization is a program the patient attends daily, usually for a set number of hours each day. The program is structured, and includes group therapy, individual therapy, family and marital therapy, patient government, and various occupational and recreational activities that provide living experience. This experience helps patients learn to cooperate with others, structure their time, and direct their efforts most effectively. It resembles employment in that the individual leaves home at a regular time each morning and returns home in the afternoon or early evening.

Partial hospitalization is offered as an alternative to hospital admission when patient health and safety do not require inpatient care. Hospital admission often becomes unnecessary when a patient becomes therapeutically involved in a partial program, such as a day treatment center.

Currently there are few partial hospitalization programs available for PTSD patients. I feel strongly that there should be many, since they would enable many patients to avoid full hospital admission, which is the most restrictive kind of treatment. It is preferable that the patient receive the least restrictive treatment, and each individual should have the full continuum of treatment available.

I will briefly describe the operation of the *Day Treatment Center* with which I was associated for a number of years. Patients were invited to attend, and since there was no good way of obliging attendance, the program had to be pleasant and attractive. This required a change from hospital staff policies that included requirements, and penalties when the requirements were not met. Therefore, a positive feedback program was seen as more attractive and therapeutically most effective. Staff members cultivated the ability to notice and provide positive feedback for all effort and achievement. The patient group was involved responsibly in this process, commending one another for positives and encouraging one another. Staff members learned to respect each individual and did not patronize patients.

The day started with a staff meeting before the patients arrived. We discussed each patient briefly, what was needed and what we would work on that day. Treatment was always individualized. Differences in opinion were resolved before they could affect treatment. In addition to patient issues, other issues or problems related to the program and policy were discussed. When the patients came in, we tried to be free of paperwork so we could give them our full attention. Incidentally, they were called *members,* rather than patients. That was part of cultivating a club atmosphere that provides status and esprit. Many programs have club type names as part of this club identification.

The first activity each day was a general meeting chaired by the president of member council. The staff served only in an advisory capacity. This was the opportunity for people to greet one another and discuss responsibly the program for the day and any special problems that had to be dealt with. All members were expected to accept their fair share of responsibilities in running the program and were held accountable by member council, rather than staff. This took the authoritarian onus off the staff, who were then free to pursue therapeutic goals and provide positive feedback. Patients learned to deal with others and accept responsibility in a friendly climate that offered help and support, along with realistic rewards for effort. This atmosphere eliminated problems with violence, even though many individuals had a history of violence.

After the general meeting there were other activities. We had daily group therapy, individual and family therapy, classes, and occupational therapy. In casual conversation at lunch or during occupational therapy, patients often talked about issues they did not bring up in formal therapy sessions. Individuals were recognized, for example, for their efforts in occupational therapy to teach other patients the skills and processes involved in woodworking and other arts and crafts activities. It is another dimension of, "You get your best help in the process of helping others." Lunches were planned by the members, who decided on the menu, collected money (also from staff members), did the shopping, cooking, and cleanup. Many activities like this enabled learning that could be applied outside the program. Field trips to the community were interesting learning experiences. One could learn appropriate behavior in a good restaurant or in a museum. The integration of treatment within activities is called *milieu therapy.*

Although a day treatment program must be tailored to the needs of a particular patient group, staff attitudes described would be appropriate in any program. For a group of PTSD patients, focus would be on those symptoms. Members of the program would be helping one another to reduce time with ruminations and to control temper. A positive feedback program with member responsibility appears to be most effective in helping individuals learn to control temper.

Partial hospitalization ends when the individual can return to outpatient visits and maintain satisfactory adjustment.

HOSPITAL TREATMENT

Hospital treatment for PTSD can be handled in various ways. With traditional hospital treatment, an upset patient is admitted to a psychiatry ward on which there are patients with various diagnoses. There may be no other PTSD patients on the ward, or there could be a couple of others. A hospital program is structured, with various activities usually including group therapy. The dose of medication can be adjusted rapidly, and structure and medication are usually very helpful in overcoming an acute episode. Opportunities to talk about specific PTSD symptoms are usually limited to individual contact with staff members. Family members, particularly the spouse, are usually invited for family therapy. This helps the acute problems and prepares for hospital discharge. Acute admissions are usually limited to a week or two, although exceptions are made when necessary.

For a number of years there have been hospital units and programs devoted strictly to PTSD. Most of these units were initially in Veterans Administration Medical Centers, but other hospitals have gradually developed such specialized units. Because PTSD causes such a profound life disturbance, admission to the units is often for a period of at least three months, although some programs last as long as six months. These programs are designed to help patients learn to deal with their symptoms and gradually restructure their lives. Most programs allow individuals to progress in specified steps. Intensive individual and group therapy are always utilized. Most PTSD patients are helped to learn better temper control. If substance abuse has been a problem, which is often the case, the individual is taught how to effectively deal with it. Some of these programs invite their graduates to return if they again feel that their control is slipping.

Like milieu therapy in a Day Treatment Program, all members and staff in a hospital PTSD unit are part of the therapeutic milieu. Individuals deal with one another in real life situations in which they learn to cooperate responsibly to accomplish tasks they have agreed upon. Each individual in the milieu must learn to negotiate with other individuals or with the entire group, and accept a fair share of the responsibilities. With the help and advice of friends, one can learn to control anger and temper, and maintain responsible behavior.

Staff members in a milieu therapy situation must be free to respond spontaneously and therapeutically during various activities and in various places with a variable number of patients present. All therapeutic responses must be consistent with what is going on in the milieu, as well as what is going on with individual patients. Nothing happens in one situation that does not have an effect on other parts of the program, so everything must fit. If a staff member intimidates an individual patient, all other patients respond. Conversely, when staff members are considerate and understanding with individuals, it affects the entire program in a positive way.

In a hospital setting, patients have contact with other staff members in addition to program therapeutic staff. They deal with food service personnel, cleaning and maintenance personnel, ward secretaries, and many others. All personnel must therefore be a constructive part of the therapeutic milieu and be aware of their contribution to the therapeutic program. Showing respect for individual patients, and trying to be pleasant and helpful is part of their job. Hostile or patronizing attitudes on the part of these staff members can damage the therapeutic program and subvert the efforts of the therapeutic staff.

APPROACHING SPECIFIC SYMPTOMS

To regain control of their lives, PTSD patients must learn to control all troublesome symptoms. This can be accomplished only by a thorough understanding of each symptom, what causes it, how it relates to other symptoms, how it relates to life issues, and then learning specific measures to deal with each symptom.

The learning process takes place everywhere. It starts in individual and group therapy, then in family and marital therapy. It continues at home in dealing with all family members. It also continues at work in coping with work pressures while interacting with other people. It also continues while walking down the street, traveling, and going to bed. Some aspects of some symptom or symptoms are at work throughout the day, and often during the night. As the learning process proceeds and new knowledge is applied, problems gradually recede and feelings of control get stronger.

During individual, group, family, and marital therapy, the control of specific symptoms is frequently discussed. During group therapy, members help one another on the basis of their own experience with a given symptom. In marital therapy, marital partners also learn to help one another with particular symptoms.

In the treatment section, the knowledge and understanding of each symptom is applied to treatment.

Chapter 44

HELPFUL SUGGESTIONS FOR TREATMENT

In the process of treating PTSD patients over the years, I found various common sense suggestions helpful. Many of these suggestions have become an integral part of treatment. They are not listed in a special order, but most suggestions are related to others.

PAGE FROM *DSM-III-R*

I make copies of the page from *DSM-III-R*, the official book of psychiatric diagnosis, in which the symptoms of PTSD are listed. I give the patient a copy to read during the first interview after I have determined that this diagnosis is likely. I then ask the patient if many of the listed symptoms are familiar. Usually the patient relates to many of them, and I explain that we will be discussing most of them. Before doing so, I ask them to read the first sentence which states, "The person has experienced an event that is outside the range of usual human experience and that would be markedly distressing to almost anyone." For the many patients who never heard of this diagnosis, who are ashamed and self-conscious about their symptoms, who may feel they are abnormal or are going crazy, I explain that the sentence means it is *normal* for them to have these symptoms, which are common following trauma. They should therefore consider themselves normal, rather than abnormal. Knowing what they suffer from and what the symptoms are, they can now feel some optimism about getting appropriate help.

It should be apparent that showing patients the official diagnosis is a way of helping their problems with stigma. They have an established diagnosis from a known cause, which means they are not abnormal or going crazy. Also, they are not different or inferior in any way, because trauma "would be markedly distressing to almost anyone." It is also a way of introducing the symptoms we will be talking about during evaluation, and then in treatment.

ROLE OF STAFF

Treatment is always most effective when transference problems are kept to a minimum. *Transference* is the term that describes our tendency to react to others in a way that is partly determined by our past experience. For example, while growing up many people developed negative feelings toward those in authority, including parents and teachers. Without realizing it, they may now have negative feelings toward the doctor, who is viewed as an authority figure, no matter what the doctor's personality. Therefore, when the doctor behaves in some way that may be perceived as authoritative, it can elicit an unexpectedly strong negative response from the patient.

I feel that such potential problems can be minimized by an approach to treatment in which the patient is taught about how things work, what causes problems, and what helps the problems. I often tell patients that I am more like a teacher, and when you learn more about how it works and what to do, you can decide what to work on and what you want to accomplish. I don't want you to do something because I said so, but because you have decided that it makes sense to you. When you get more practice in knowing how to avoid problems and how to deal with them, your ability to stay in control and accomplish what you want will gradually improve. Patients are in this way provided specific tasks to work on that will relieve specific problems.

This approach to treatment has several advantages. It keeps transference problems to a minimum, and the therapist is always clearly on the side of the patient, wanting them to succeed and achieve their goals (not your goals). Patients remain responsible and avoid the "here I am, cure me" problem. The issue of the patient regaining control is always clearly involved. It enables a step by step approach in which progress is identified, adding a sense of optimism, elevating self-esteem, overcoming helplessness, and providing the therapist ample opportunities to provide positive feedback. In addition, by reminding patients that they made progress by virtue of their own efforts, they are given credit and can take pride in their achievements. This motivates additional effort toward achieving goals, and helps patients feel good about themselves. Patients get credit for success, not the staff. However, patients appreciate the staff role in this process.

This approach also keeps the patient responsible for the success of treatment. The harder they work on it, the greater the success. The approach also encourages independence from treatment as rapidly as possible, rather than dependence on treatment.

REMEMBER THAT PROGRESS IS GRADUAL

It is always important to remember that progress in treatment is gradual and takes time. Patients often become impatient with themselves when problems persist or recur as a result of increased specific triggers or increased stress. Progressing step by step is a concept that patients often need to be reminded of. Patients often tell one another that you have to crawl before you can walk, and you have to walk before you can run.

Where the patient starts from is an important part of tailoring treatment to individual needs. By this I mean that PTSD patients often begin less accessible to treatment than patients with many other diagnoses. When they start treatment they often have so many strong emotions and preoccupations (and ruminations) churning around that they may actually hear little of what is said. This appears to be an aspect of the "difficulty concentrating" symptom. I will use a typical example. Since I encourage PTSD patients to help one another on the basis of their own experience, I have often asked a new patient if he or she would be interested in talking to another patient with longer experience in treatment. I did this recently with two Vietnam veterans. After they talked for a time, I later spoke to the man who had derived much help from treatment. He said of the new man, "He wasn't listening, he hardly heard a word I said. He didn't pay any more attention than I did when I first started." He was obviously aware of the new patient's inability to focus well in treatment initially, which is another factor increasing the time it takes to benefit from treatment. An adequate dose of antidepressant medication is often helpful for this problem.

FOCUS ON REDUCING RUMINATIONS

Maintaining focus on reducing ruminations as the key to successfully overcoming the symptoms of PTSD is helpful in a number of ways. Since total time with ruminations daily is related to the intensity of all symptoms and problems, working on reducing such *bad time* can help any problem. The individual is never helpless because there is always something definite to work on that will help.

Since time with ruminations can be reduced only gradually, patients can be coached at all times on such things as reducing triggers, ways of catching ruminations faster, and ways of applying concentration. Ability to do these things needs constant work and improvement, which places responsibility on the patient to work at them in order to obtain relief. Since the process is viewed as gradual, one need not feel like a failure if all problems are not quickly resolved. I often say things like, "If you are ruminating for an average of ten hours a day, you may cut it to seven or eight hours as a first step. Although that's an improvement, it is still far too much bad time. However, you don't go from ten hours a day to two hours a day in the first step."

Catching ruminations early, preferably as soon as they start, is the goal that gives two advantages. It is much easier to *switch channels* and get your concentration elsewhere when it first starts. After ruminating for a period of time, you get progressively more upset and it is harder to break away. The second advantage of catching it quickly is that it effectively reduces the total time spent with ruminations.

Progress and improved control are therefore gradual, with many small successes and improvements along the way. This provides opportunities for positive feedback by staff and other group members, which boosts confidence and morale and fights discouragement. All individuals are encouraged to learn to give themselves positive feedback for their accomplishments.

DEALING WITH HELPLESSNESS

Dealing with helplessness and nurturing a growing sense of control is always a focus of treatment, since it is such an important issue. It was just described above in reviewing the role of staff. Helplessness is dealt with by helping patients learn to prevent problems, or cope with them more effectively when they occur. An example would be the problem of ruminations. Patients learn to reduce the frequency of ruminations by learning to avoid triggers. When ruminations occur, their impact is greatly reduced by catching them quickly and applying concentration.

Patients are therefore given tools to work with. They learn what to do and how to do it in dealing with various symptoms and problems. This is often referred to as *homework*. As they gradually learn to control problems, and know what to do in various situations, the increased sense of control gradually diminishes feelings of helplessness.

BUILD ON SUCCESS

The principle of building on success to achieve greater success applies to many areas of life. It is obviously used in the above suggestions for treatment for ruminations. Success to some degree in the patient's efforts to cope with their problems boosts confidence and further motivates them to work harder to make more progress. The methods and abilities used to solve one problem can be used to solve other problems. These can be referred to as *tools* that one can work with.

POSITIVE FEEDBACK

Positive feedback is generally accepted as the most successful method of learning, whether one is learning arithmetic or how to deal more effectively with problems. In this method, recognition and reward (praise, prizes) are given for positive effort and achievement, or what the individual does or accomplishes. *Negative feedback* is punishment for mistakes, or what the individual doesn't do or does wrong.

When patients are learning to cope with their problems, the therapist therefore looks for and gives recognition to successful efforts of any type. For example, this can be done when patients learn to avoid specific triggers or catch ruminations faster.

OBJECTIVE DECISIONS

Most people understand that objective decisions are better than subjective decisions. *Objective decisions* are made by thinking clearly with a cool head. *Subjective decisions* are those made on the basis of emotion, usually before thinking. For example, people who lose their temper often regret it afterwards. They must learn that if they can think clearly first, their decisions will be more objective and they will do what they really prefer. When you jump before you think, you usually pay a price. The price can become very high.

Whether dealing with temper or any other life problem, I always encourage patients to think clearly before acting to decide what they want and what they don't. Only then can someone be in good control.

KEEPING BALANCE

Most people pay more attention to negatives than to positives. We all learn to do this from an early age. A child, for example, can do a hundred right things and then make one mistake. It is the mistake that is apt to be the focus for parents and teachers. This problem also exists in the workplace.

People who are depressed tend to focus on negatives more than average, and of course all PTSD patients are depressed. I therefore point out to PTSD patients that there are always good and positive things in life, and always some bad and negative things. When we get into the habit of seeing only the negatives and forget about the positives, we lose balance. Then everything seems to be bad. We therefore must start reminding ourselves about the positives when we recognize that happening, so we can see the whole picture more objectively and keep a balance in our lives. When the balance is lost, it makes us more depressed. If we keep reminding ourselves about the positives, we can get into the habit of seeing the entire picture and avoid undue depression. This is another way of using our intelligence to help ourselves and to maintain objectivity.

ANY HABIT CAN BE CHANGED

Seeing only negatives is a habit that people can get into that works against them and against their best interests. We are not born with these habits, but acquire them as we go through life. Fortunately, any habit can be changed if we work on it.

When these habits work against our best interests, we can benefit by changing them. Habits are not changed without work, because they sneak up on us. Habits are the things we find ourselves doing without thinking about it. Therefore, thinking about it and catching it quickly enables us to gradually change the habit that works against us. It takes time, and it is never easy. However, the results of such efforts are very worthwhile.

MAKING POSITIVES OUT OF NEGATIVES

Making mistakes is a normal part of learning. Everybody makes mistakes, and we often learn best from our mistakes.

In our culture, this natural aspect of learning is usually not allowed.

Making a mistake becomes a cardinal sin. In school, for example, making a mistake can provoke the anger of teachers and then of parents. Some children become afraid to try for fear of making mistakes. Most of us react too strongly to mistakes, particularly our own mistakes.

When the PTSD patients start working on problems, they can make mistakes. Instead of doing what they really want, old habits sneak in and they do something different in many instances. They react to this by becoming discouraged and self critical. That makes them more depressed and increases ruminations.

To help with such problems, I like to use baseball analogies. When you first swing at the ball, you don't hit a home run. You probably don't even touch it. After lots of practice and hard work, you can start getting some base hits. It takes time before you start hitting home runs. This is likewise true when you start work on changing a habit.

Most people are familiar with the name of Babe Ruth and that he held the record for home runs. However, he held another record, the record for the most strikeouts. I make the point that if he had allowed those strikeouts to make him depressed and discouraged, he would have never hit the home runs.

In working on your problems, you'll make some home runs after a time, but you'll also strike out. If you have a bad experience or make a mistake, don't allow it to become a tragedy. Use the mistake as an opportunity to learn something important, so you don't keep making the same mistake. Next time a similar problem comes up, you will handle it in a way you would prefer. That is the way to use mistakes in a positive manner, as opportunities to learn and grow. Don't let mistakes get you down. I often say, "Don't get sad, get mad." Strengthen your resolve to deal better with your mistakes so you can make positives out of negatives.

Here again I sometimes use my personal experience to illustrate. When I was spending a great deal of time with ruminations, I became aware that the longer they lasted, the more upset I felt. I therefore reasoned that if I could cut them short, it would help. I then determined that I would catch them sooner, preferably when they first started.

Despite my good plan, I would often suddenly realize that I had been spending the last couple of hours ruminating. That got me angry, not discouraged, and I vowed to do better next time. I would think about what went on during the past half hour or hour, looking for earlier clues like feeling upset, anxiety felt in a particular area, or depression. This approach enabled me to gradually learn cues that I could pick up earlier and earlier, progressively reducing the time spent with ruminations. Since the ruminations were so upsetting, I worked very hard at this process. It took time, but I was finally able to detect the instant the rumination first started. By making my reaction to this instantaneous, I was able to cut the time with ruminations to zero. When I was able to do that consistently, my problems with PTSD were over.

THE IMPORTANCE OF A REGULAR SCHEDULE

Most people suffering from serious symptoms of PTSD don't feel well most of the time, don't sleep well, and have difficulty doing the things they want to do. They can learn to stop doing the things that make them feel worse and start doing the things that help them feel better.

I explain that an important part of getting to feel better is to get on a regular schedule. If you eat at a given time each day, for example, you get hungry at that time each day. Your body becomes accustomed to that schedule since we have a body clock.

In the same manner, you will sleep better when you are in bed during the same hours each night. A change of just one hour, when the time changes to daylight savings time, disturbs the body clock, and most people don't feel right for a week or so. Changing your bedtime an hour or more from one day to the next gives you jet lag. I often say, "You can't feel good if you keep doing things that make you feel bad." Keeping a regular time to get up in the morning and go to bed at night allows you to sleep better. Your body then knows when to sleep. It is best to avoid doing things that will cause body clock problems for sleep. Therefore, avoid taking naps during the day. If you get up at night to go to the bathroom or sip some water, go right back to bed. Don't stay up just because you are awake, but return to bed. If you wake up at 3:00 AM each morning and stay out of bed for a while, you will start waking up at that time each morning.

In addition to regular time to go to bed and regular time to get up in the morning, it is best to eat meals at regular times each day. That makes for better appetite, better digestion, and fewer problems with hunger and between meal snacks that may cause weight problems.

Many PTSD patients are concerned about their weight. Some want to gain, but most want to lose weight. I suggest that the best way to control weight is to plan meals ahead. When planning meals, you must plan on getting good nutrition, which is possible with a lower caloric intake. We talk during treatment about aspects of healthy diet and cooking unless the patient already has that knowledge. We talk about the importance of planning portion size, since it is not only what you eat, but how much. Old habits of portion size or foods high in fats and oils must be guarded against. When the menu is made out a week or more ahead of time, shopping is simplified. I remind patients that when you go into a food store hungry, you do more impulse buying of junk food. In the same way, when you walk into the kitchen hungry and with no fixed menu, you start grabbing for things that may not fit with your diet plan. Such menu planning has enabled many of my patients to accomplish their objectives of weight loss or gain. Planning ahead gives one better control.

Most people feel much better when they exercise regularly. Therefore, I encourage everyone to get on a regular exercise program as another way of feeling better. Regular exercise not only helps you feel better and improves general health, but also gives you more energy. In addition, when you are trying to lose weight, diet is far more effective when combined with regular exercise. It is much more difficult to lose weight permanently on diet alone.

Regular exercise means exercise on most days, not a couple of times per week. I suggest exercise on five or six days per week. Unless you build a time for exercise into your schedule it is often hard to find the time for it. Having a companion to exercise with can make it more pleasant and easier to stick to.

The most beneficial exercise is an aerobic activity that keeps the heart beating faster, keeps breathing deeper, and the blood circulating faster continuously for at least a half hour. Walking is one of the best exercises, and a brisk walk gives as much aerobic benefit as jogging, without the pounding. Swimming is also a good exercise, and some people prefer to swim on some exercise days, or every time. Others prefer an aerobics class for their exercise.

I usually suggest that everyone consult their family doctor before starting an exercise program in order to avoid physical risks. Even when someone is young and in good shape, conditioning should be gradual. If one has hypertension, heart problems or diabetes, for example, medical recommendations regarding exercise are even more important.

When someone starts walking, they should not walk so far that they become overly tired. Walk a short distance for a week or more before increasing the distance. As time goes by, distance and speed can usually be increased gradually. I tell my patients that if they walk a brisk three miles daily, that is sufficient to maintain full aerobic benefit. Some prefer to walk even further when conditioned because they enjoy it, and of course it is not a problem as long as they work up to it gradually.

RELAXATION

We live in a tense and hectic world in which it is difficult for most people to relax. Those suffering from PTSD have added tension from spending time ruminating, plus trying to cope with their various symptoms. Finding ways to relax is therefore important to maintain health. Learning to relax is another way in which you can help yourself feel better.

A very helpful method of relaxing is called *progressive muscular relaxation*. Since it is not possible to relax unless breathing is controlled, I explain and demonstrate that relaxed breathing is the type of breathing we observe when someone is sleeping. Inspiration is fairly deep and relatively brief. Expiration is prolonged. I suggest that patients take a deep breath while in the office, and then see how long they can keep expiring. I explain that it takes time and practice to make expiration take longer, and to get all the air out.

When starting a period of progressive muscular relaxation, lie comfortably in bed on your back with eyes closed, arms at your side, and head back without a pillow. Keep the shoulders down, since hunching up the shoulders keeps you tense and decreases your lung capacity. When comfortable, start with a good deep breath, then let it out slowly, and let it all out before taking another breath. You can breathe deeper by using the diaphragm, so when you breathe deeply, feel your abdomen rise. Some people call it *belly breathing*. After taking a few deep breaths and letting them out slowly, you should start to relax.

It is proven fact that you can relax a muscle or a group of muscles by concentrating on them to relax. You can gradually learn to concentrate on relaxing muscles during each extended expiration. As soon as expiration starts, concentrate on the muscles in your toes relaxing. With the next breath, concentrate on the muscles in the feet relaxing. Next breath the muscles around the ankle, then the lower leg, knees, thigh, hips, and gradually upward. When you get to the shoulders, next comes the upper arm, elbow, lower arm, wrist, hand, and fingers. Don't forget the neck muscles that can get very tense, muscles in face and head, and of course the tongue. If a given group of muscles don't feel sufficiently relaxed, give them an extra breath or two. There is no hurry, no deadline. When you have relaxed every group of muscles, start over again at the toes if still awake.

Practice relaxation when going to bed at night, when awakening in bed during the night, and one or more times during the day if you can get the privacy to lie down for ten or fifteen minutes. It will help. Remember that you improve with practice, so gradually you will get more relaxed with this technique, and relax more quickly. Initially it may take some time doing this before you start feeling relaxed.

During the day at various times you may become aware that you are tense and not breathing well. Even if you are driving or at the office, you can start taking a few deep breaths, let them out slowly, and feel your muscles relax. That can help break the tension without attracting the attention of other people.

Progressive muscular relaxation has benefits in addition to helping you relax. When you go to bed at night, there is a tendency for thoughts to wander, with the possibility of starting ruminations that will certainly keep you awake. However, if you remain relaxed but keep concentrating on breathing and relaxing groups of muscles, you get to sleep free of the danger of ruminations or any other upsetting thoughts or memories.

Some people have experience using relaxation tapes to get relaxed, and prefer them to using progressive muscular relaxation. I don't object to their use as long as they accomplish relaxation and maintain concentration in a way that prevents ruminations.

SERENITY PRAYER

God grant me the serenity to accept the things I cannot change, courage to change the things I can, and the wisdom to know the difference.

This simple but powerful serenity prayer has been popularized over the years by Alcoholics Anonymous, and applies to many everyday problems in life. PTSD patients often keep getting upset about things they can't change, and the serenity prayer can be a helpful reminder. Examples of things people repeatedly get upset about that can't be changed include their physical disability, the existence of various problems in the world, or the habits and personalities of others. For instance, I talk to many patients who frequently get upset about the behavior of another person, whether it be a family member, business associate, or friend. I keep reminding them that there is only one person they can control and change. They may prefer that another person changes, but they have no control of others, only of themselves. Therefore, repeatedly becoming upset by the behavior of another person does nothing constructive. In fact, the stress of such concerns and upsets tends to increase ruminations for the PTSD patient. All factors that increase stress are therefore undesirable, since they tend to increase symptoms.

The serenity prayer is therefore a helpful reminder for many PTSD patients. For this reason, I keep business cards with the prayer on my desk. I encourage patients to carry the cards or keep them in locations where they can serve as helpful reminders.

Chapter 45

TREATMENT OF ACUTE PTSD SYMPTOMS

By definition, acute PTSD includes symptoms lasting six months or less. When symptoms last longer than six months, it is considered to be *chronic or prolonged PTSD.*

Treatment of acute symptoms, or *early intervention,* is best started as soon as possible after the trauma.[3] Immediately afterwards is most effective. In Chapter 40 we reviewed the prevention of long-term symptoms. The first step is *debriefing,* or the opportunity to describe and discuss what happened with a sympathetic, understanding listener. The listener is preferably someone who has been through similar experiences, and therefore felt by the patient to be capable of fully understanding all aspects of the problem and of their feelings. For any individual, debriefing is most effective when it takes place in the company of all others who just went through the same traumatic experience. When the trauma was suffered alone, initial debriefing involves only the victim and the sympathetic listener.

The next step after debriefing is *discussion,* in groups of ten to twelve individuals, led by a sympathetic listener who is also a trained group therapist. When a large group of people have suffered trauma together, such as in a flood or storm, they must be divided into smaller groups for discussion. The individual who suffered trauma alone, such as a rape victim, should be placed in a group with ten to twelve other rape victims.

Small groups should meet at least weekly for further discussion of the trauma and for mutual support. Meetings should continue until everyone feels that the group is no longer necessary. Such groups may meet two or three times and decide to terminate treatment. Other groups may feel the need to continue longer. Generally, the more quickly after trauma the process is started, the faster and easier the treatment. After completion of this group process, it is highly unlikely that any participants will encounter further problems with PTSD.

In addition to group therapy, individual therapy and family therapy must be included. They are described in Chapters 40 and 43.

Starting in World War I, military physicians learned that sending a soldier with acute PTSD symptoms to long term hospital treatment frequently resulted in long term symptoms and disability. However, they also learned that giving the stricken soldier a few days of rest with humane and understanding medical personnel and fellow soldiers allowed return to the combat unit and prevention of long-term symptoms. The brief rest from combat just described would have been even more effective if it included debriefing and other aspects of prevention already described. This general approach to dealing with acute symptoms can be compared to getting back up on the horse that just threw you, or going back up in an airplane after surviving a crash.

The treatment of chronic or prolonged PTSD is necessarily longer and more comprehensive. It will be reviewed in the pages that follow.

Chapter 46

"RECURRENT AND INTRUSIVE DISTRESSING RECOLLECTIONS OF THE EVENT"

In describing this most important symptom, we reviewed how it is central to PTSD. We also reviewed the distinction between recollections, memories, and ruminations. Ruminations are by far the most disturbing. The more time spent reexperiencing the trauma, the greater the intensity of all other symptoms on the list, the greater the suffering, distress, and disruption of one's life, the greater the impact on physical health, and the stronger the feelings of helplessness and hopelessness. Learning to control the many aspects of this symptom is therefore an essential aspect of all treatment, starting with the first visit.

One of the first steps for patients is learning they are not alone or going crazy, that others have similar symptoms resulting from trauma. This is learned best in group therapy, where the individual hears others talking about it. They learn that they are usually not aware of drifting into a rumination, that they are not conscious of the experience, and if someone asked them what they were thinking about they would probably say, "Nothing." However, one can learn to be aware of the results of ruminations to tell them it is going on. They can become aware of bodily sensations unique for each individual, such as feeling anxious or tremulous, feeling depressed with or without crying, a nervous or sinking feeling in the pit of the stomach, GI upset or headache, and so on. They learn that with practice and effort it is possible to catch it faster and faster, gradually reducing total time with ruminations. To the extent that total time per day spent ruminating is reduced, symptoms become fewer and less severe.

Reducing time with ruminations is learned in steps. The first step is reducing triggers for the traumatic experience. Triggers can be specific reminders. Examples would be a war veteran watching a military parade, an accident victim observing a serious highway accident, or a rape victim watching a movie or TV show about rape. It is important for

PTSD patients to learn to avoid triggers as one way of reducing the traumatic time spent ruminating.

There are also indirect specific triggers that must be recognized and avoided. Indirect triggers could be sight of the ocean for a flood victim, a particular model or color of car for an accident victim, or a river or lake for a Vietnam veteran. Anything that triggers ruminations must be avoided or kept to a minimum.

Another type of indirect trigger is behavior related to the trauma. For example, after a mugging or rape, the victim often develops hypervigilance that can serve as a trigger for the memory. A war veteran who is driving and automatically looking for hiding places near the road, or possible gun emplacement sites is likewise triggering ruminations. I tell these people they must stop playing *war games* that increase the rumination problem and the total time spent in this manner. Reducing total daily rumination time is always a priority in treatment.

Stress from any source is another indirect trigger, increasing the rumination problem. The stress can be financial problems and worries, marital problems, a sick child, physical illness, or pain. An overactive thyroid gland can be the stress. I have known many individuals who did not have serious symptoms of PTSD until they developed a chronic pain problem. Chronic severe pain is a stress, and therefore a common trigger for greatly increased time with ruminations.

Learning to be aware of ruminations more quickly usually takes time and practice, since one is not consciously aware that it is occurring. One simply starts ruminating without realizing it, and can spend long periods of time in this manner. It can last an hour or two at a time, or for many hours. The longer the period of time one repeatedly relives a traumatic event, the greater the tension, anger, and other symptoms.

Identifying the start of a rumination is important, because terminating it quickly avoids the cumulative trauma of spending a long time with it. In addition, if you catch it at the start, it is not difficult to get concentration elsewhere. The longer people are ruminating, the more upset they get, and the more difficult it is to break away from the rumination.

I explain to patients that you can't stop thinking of things, but you can learn to control the time spent with a thought or memory. I review the fact that the severity of symptoms depends on the total time spent with ruminations, that the more the bad time is reduced, the fewer the symptoms, and the better they will feel. Reducing rumination time is therefore always important in treatment, since all other symptoms of PTSD improve when the bad time is reduced. I also use the example of prisoners of war. Those who did not learn to tune out the horrors by spending much of their time with pleasant thoughts and memories often gave up and simply died.

As people become more aware of their bodily feelings, they can gradually learn to become aware of ruminations more quickly. I encourage such learning in steps. If one becomes aware of ruminations only when they are losing their temper or having a bad headache, I suggest that they think about any feeling of anxiety or depression prior to that. When an earlier sign is recognized, I suggest searching for a still earlier signal. The goal is to consistently catch ruminations the instant they start, completely eliminating time spent with them. This process is always stressed in treatment because it is the single most helpful thing one can learn to do to obtain relief, since all other symptoms appear to be energized by the time spent with ruminations.

The importance of catching ruminations instantly is a theme I repeat often during treatment. Catching them the instant they start makes it easier to get away from them, and no time is spent with a rumination. At times I find a military example helpful to a patient's understanding of the concept. For example, I was treating a Vietnam veteran who remained in service after his return from the war. He then had a long career in military intelligence, where he was often in life-threatening situations. He survived because he developed the ability to react instantly and appropriately to various threats. Since he was having difficulty catching ruminations quickly, I suggested that he use his military training. That training helped him learn to react instantly. In this instance, he must learn a similar instantaneous reaction to the start of a rumination.

As soon as one is aware of ruminating, they must learn to quickly switch channels and get their concentration elsewhere. (This process is referred to by some as *thought stopping*). They must learn that nobody can concentrate fully on more than one thing at a time. That is why they can't concentrate on reading, since their concentration is on reliving a past traumatic experience. Therefore, by applying concentration to another activity, ruminations can be forced out. I often give patients my personal example. When I returned to college with the intention of going to medical school, I had difficulty concentrating on studies. That alarmed me, since inability to study would spell failure for my career plans. I therefore fought hard to force my concentration onto the book. I worked and worked at fighting to get concentration until I finally got better at it. My gradually learning to keep my concentration where I wanted it ended up helping me a great deal, since it became a way of cutting off and controlling ruminations. At the time I didn't understand the process, but I do now.

Many of my patients learn to use reading as a way of fighting off ruminations, and it is one good way. It is a gradual process and takes a great deal of effort. Reading material should be interesting for the individual, but books with triggers must be avoided. War or violence are examples of possible problems, and for many, books with these subjects are best avoided.

Activity of any type that requires concentration can be used in this manner. Routine tasks that do not require concentration can allow the mind to wander. A wandering mind often results in ruminations. When discussing activities an individual will use to achieve and maintain concentration, I suggest that they be interesting and enjoyable. If a woman wants to crochet as an activity, I inquire about the concentration required. I have learned that there are types of crocheting that indeed require full concentration. Model making and radio kit building can do it for some and not for others. Many of those fighting PTSD symptoms find that physical activity helps them feel better and is most helpful in maintaining concentration. I have known patients who worked on their car, worked with animals, did woodworking, or other shop tasks, rearranged furniture or the contents of drawers, or anything else that requires concentration. Here again, triggers must be avoided, like placing weapons on a model airplane or listening to a radio scanner. If someone decides to work on a model airplane, for example, I would suggest avoiding a warplane of any kind for the combat veteran.

I often use an example from personal experience in dealing with triggers. I presently live near a large military reservation. When large size artillery shells are fired, which at times can be frequently throughout the day, the sound can carry for many miles, and the shock wave can rattle windows. There was a time when this sound could upset me and start ruminations. One day I finally told myself, "You're still reacting like they're trying to kill you." I realized I must reduce my reaction to this sound. I told myself that those sounds are now part of training in which fire is aimed at a safe area. They are not trying to kill anybody, but attempt to avoid injuring anyone. The sound is therefore not a threat to me. Following this reasoning, I would immediately tell myself, "They're training," whenever I heard the sound, and try to maintain concentration on what I was doing. When I was finally able to do this instantly, such a sound no longer caused me to spend time with ruminations. Even though I still don't care for the sound, it doesn't affect me because I react promptly and maintain concentration.

Additional help in recognizing the start of ruminations more quickly can be obtained from an understanding spouse, family member or friend. I tell patients, "Another person can spot when you are someplace else, not here, and tell you." One of the common problems in doing this is the tendency for the patient to get angry when reminded. I have known men who gave their wives a terrible time for their attempts to help. This is a subject often discussed in marital therapy. The patient must learn to moderate angry responses in order to receive this important help. Anything that reduces time with ruminations must be recognized as important in the process of getting well.

Another tip I often suggest for people having difficulty recognizing the ruminations is to try reading. I say, "If you try to read and can't concentrate on it, that should tell you what is happening." I therefore suggest that attempting to read every so often during the day can be a helpful way to check it out.

When the patient suddenly becomes aware of ruminating, strong feelings and emotions can make clear thinking difficult. That is not the time to try to decide what can be done to apply concentration. I strongly advise patients to always have something ready at hand when needed. If it is reading, have books in strategic places with a bookmark in the page, so you can get right to it. A prompt response not only reduces rumination time. By responding sooner, rather than later, the task is less difficult. Plans for applying concentration in order to end a rumination must be made beforehand with a clear head.

Another suggestion to maintain concentration is something I learned to do when I had the problem. When driving, for example, it is easy for the mind to wander. I started concentrating, while driving, on makes and models of other cars, on license plates, unusual car or truck features, on buildings or any other objects in the landscape. While walking along I would concentrate on buildings, shape, size, types of windows, or any other unique features I could find. When walking outside of the city, I would notice types of trees, texture of bark, shape of leaves, flowers or shrubs, birds, and other forms of wildlife. I shared this with many patients who learned to get into this habit with benefit. Keeping the mind occupied is a good protection against slipping into ruminations.

When I first explain these issues to some PTSD patients, they say they always felt better when busy. They therefore often kept busy in the past and did not recognize why it helped them, perhaps for a number of years.

An important aspect of learning to deal more effectively with ruminations is learning from experience. For example, if a patient has a bad day with much rumination time, I encourage viewing each rumination episode as a learning experience. I ask questions like, "What do you think started it? Can you think of any events or feelings that you could have recognized sooner to know you were ruminating?" By such efforts, patients start getting into the habit of more often recognizing that stress or a specific trigger are at work, to then be on guard to prevent or catch the start of ruminations early. Persistent efforts to recognize one's emotions and bodily feelings that indicate ruminations are one of the most important ways to reduce symptoms and problems. It is easy to get away from the rumination when it first starts, but gets harder as time goes by. Learning to catch ruminations earlier is important. By using such experiences to learn, one can gradually get better at catching ruminations early; the earlier, the better. When a PTSD patient comes in discouraged over having a bad day of ruminations and a feeling of loss of control, I usually say, "Don't get sad, get mad. Get determination that you will learn something from each episode that can prevent or reduce the same problems when something similar comes up in the future. There's nothing wrong with making a mistake if you learn from it, and if you don't keep making the same mistakes."

When a patient is first presented with the task of recognizing ruminations and quickly applying concentration, the prospects of success are often daunting. To encourage someone to work at the task gradually, I frequently use baseball analogies. When you first swing at the ball, you will probably miss it. However, with practice you will start to hit it some of the time. After more practice, you will start getting some base hits. It takes time before you start hitting home runs.

Chapter 47

"RECURRENT DISTRESSING DREAMS OF THE EVENT"

The importance of awakening fully from a nightmare, and as quickly as possible, has already been discussed. Since it is often difficult to awaken completely, the individual can continue the nightmare while becoming physically active, and not recall afterward what happened.[4] We gave examples like attacking the spouse in bed, or getting up to do various things that are not remembered in the morning.

It helps for the individual to be aware of the importance of awakening quickly. If that is firmly in mind, it can be remembered and acted upon while one is only partly awake. Keeping a light on in the bedroom also helps, because the person trying to awaken can look at familiar objects in the bedroom. Some people keep an illuminated digital clock with large numbers at the bedside to help the effort of becoming oriented more quickly.

Keeping a light on helps another aspect of the awakening problems. While one is only partly awake and a frightening nightmare continues, many people open their eyes and see or look for frightening people or objects. With adequate light, they can quickly reassure themselves that nobody is there. Darkness in the room makes it more difficult to deal with this particular aspect of the problem.

A spouse can be very helpful, but must learn to be careful. The wives of many war veterans, for example, were often pounded or strangled when they tried to awaken their husbands from a nightmare. A spouse must keep at a safe distance while trying to awaken the patient, by shouting and possibly by using a soft pole or roll of paper as a prod. Husband and wife can also agree beforehand on special words to be used in the process, such as "Wake up," "Stop," or any word the patient can recognize as part of the need to awaken fully.

As soon as possible, when sufficiently awake, the patient should get out of bed and start moving and walking to awaken more completely.

Getting a drink of water or soda can help the process. Talking to one's spouse is often helpful. A person should remain out of bed and active until there is no question that they are completely awake. This is important because if not fully awake, the nightmare continues. If the patient returns to bed before awakening is complete, they simply continue the nightmare. Full awakening is necessary to terminate the nightmare. Many of those with PTSD sleep in a separate bedroom out of concern that they could hurt their spouse or do something they regret while only partially awake after a nightmare. They do various things to help themselves awaken faster. I have known individuals who tie an ankle or toe to a bedpost, or ring a loud bell or alarm if they get out of bed. For example, a loud cowbell could be attached to a cord or to the bedroom door. Opening the door rings the bell and awakens the patient.

After the patient is completely awake, the next step is relaxing. People do various things during the night to relax after a nightmare and get their thoughts away from the nightmare. They talk to their understanding spouse, watch TV or read, etc. When watching TV or reading, triggers must be avoided. When sufficiently relaxed, the individual can return to bed with reasonable expectation of getting back to sleep.

Of course it is better to avoid nightmares than to deal with them after they occur. The most effective way to accomplish this is by reducing the time spent with ruminations during the day, since we tend to dream about things that have been on our mind while awake. Patients therefore always know what to work on to reduce the nightmare problem.

Another problem that tends to increase nightmares is reminders or ruminations just before going to sleep. For example, many individuals are in the habit of watching news on TV before going to bed. If a trigger is encountered at that time, it is more likely to result in a nightmare that night than if it happened earlier in the day. Likewise, lying in bed with one's mind wandering can have similar results. I therefore encourage relaxation exercises at bedtime to reduce that problem.

Chapter 48

"SUDDEN ACTION OR FEELING AS IF THE TRAUMATIC EVENT WERE RECURRING (INCLUDES A SENSE OF RELIVING THE EXPERIENCE, ILLUSIONS, HALLUCINATIONS, AND DISSOCIATIVE 'FLASHBACK' EPISODES, EVEN THOSE THAT OCCUR UPON AWAKENING OR WHEN INTOXICATED)"

This is the classical *flashback* that can occur without warning during waking hours. The individual suddenly starts reliving a traumatic episode, and displays behavior appropriate for that episode. This symptom is rare, and over the years I have never seen a PTSD patient with this symptom.

The only treatment possible for such an episode would be the same as for the patient who has not fully awakened from a nightmare, and is displaying behavior appropriate to the traumatic event. In that instance, full awakening as soon as possible was described as the way to terminate the problem. Therefore, I think a similar approach could be used to terminate the flashback.

Prevention is obviously the best way of dealing with this type of problem. I therefore feel that reducing time with ruminations, as always, would be very helpful. Individual and group therapy could help to improve awareness of triggers. Medication can also be helpful.[5]

Chapter 49

"INTENSE PSYCHOLOGICAL DISTRESS AT EXPOSURE TO EVENTS THAT SYMBOLIZE OR RESEMBLE AN ASPECT OF THE TRAUMATIC EVENT, INCLUDING ANNIVERSARIES OF THE TRAUMA"

Since exposure to events that symbolize or resemble an aspect of the traumatic event can be a trigger for ruminations, such events must be avoided if possible. As the individual learns in individual and group therapy to recognize more of these things, gradual reduction in frequency and intensity of the problems is possible. When the problem is not avoided and ruminations begin, catching it quickly and applying concentration elsewhere also provides relief.

The same holds true for anniversary reactions. First, the entire problem is reduced when one is able to reduce time with ruminations. Treatment improves awareness of anniversary reactions so they can be avoided, caught faster, and the effects gradually reduced. Here again, catching the rumination quickly and applying concentration elsewhere is also important. When you expect something, you can be better prepared to deal with it. That can also be true for anniversary reactions.

Chapter 50

"EFFORTS TO AVOID THOUGHTS
OR FEELINGS ASSOCIATED
WITH THE TRAUMA"

People often come to avoid thoughts or feelings without understanding the reason for doing so. Once they enter treatment, an understanding of the process gradually increases. When aware of the various thoughts and feelings that can trigger ruminations, patients become better able to control triggers and consequent ruminations. Triggers are often discussed in therapy, as well as ways to catch the start of ruminations faster and start concentrating on another activity promptly.

An example would be someone who developed PTSD after experiencing a hurricane. Such a person may find that thoughts about the weather or the possibility of a storm can trigger ruminations. They can learn to catch this quickly and *switch channels* to get their concentration elsewhere. In treatment, people gradually improve their ability to recognize potential triggers, and know what to do promptly to avoid problems.

Chapter 51

"EFFORTS TO AVOID ACTIVITIES OR SITUATIONS THAT AROUSE RECOLLECTION OF THE TRAUMA"

This symptom is related to the preceding symptom. Treatment helps people learn as many activities and situations as possible that may be triggers, and learn to avoid them more consistently. They also learn to be more alert to the start of ruminations, and know what to do promptly in order to keep bad time to a minimum.

In the preceding discussion of symptoms I reviewed the perverse aspects of this problem in which people may continue the very activities that cause the most problems. These individuals are sometimes persuaded in group to change behavior. However, when they have done these things for years, change is difficult to achieve.

I used the word "consistently" above because progress in these matters is gradual. Many times an individual forgets and suffers the consequences. For example, someone may come into a Vietnam veteran group, reporting that he's been upset. He relates that when a friend invited him to go fishing, he was enthused and went. However, getting out on a lake in a boat was a trigger that started ruminations. From this group discussion, he and others in the group with similar triggers learned to avoid fishing.

The more one learns about triggers in treatment, often through bitter personal experience, the better the ability to avoid potential triggers and consequent time with ruminations.

Chapter 52

"INABILITY TO RECALL AN IMPORTANT ASPECT OF THE TRAUMA (PSYCHOGENIC AMNESIA)"

Those suffering from PTSD usually have some degree of amnesia, and in some instances there can be amnesia for the entire traumatic episode. The individual is often aware that sections of time are blank, and may learn about what happened later from others who were present at the time. I have talked to many war veterans who had such experiences when talking to friends at a later date. During treatment I use my personal example of a blank five days, after which I "woke up" in a hospital. I learned that it was exactly five days from the medical chart. I later learned from survivors of my unit that I was talking and awake at least part of the five days. For a number of years it bothered me that there was a blank five days I could not remember. I later learned that amnesia can be protective, and asked myself why I should insist upon remembering five days that were undoubtedly terrible. I gradually changed, and became pleased and happy that I don't remember that traumatic period of time. The things I do remember from that time are bad enough.

When I talk to PTSD patients who are troubled about one or more periods of amnesia, I tell them to count their blessings. I go on to explain why, and often use my own experience as an example. Most people can accept this, and are gradually able to reduce their concern about amnesia.

For those who are concerned that amnesia could be a sign of "losing my mind," I reassure them by showing them the *DSM-III-R* list of symptoms. I go on to explain that a degree of amnesia is usual and expected with PTSD, and is therefore nothing to be concerned about. It is normal, rather than abnormal. I also remind them that not remembering some portion of the trauma is a positive rather than a negative.

Some examples of amnesia are best not talked about. The woman who recalls frightening beatings as a child from an alcoholic father often denies that sexual abuse occurred. Even when I believe sexual abuse was a good possibility, I do not always tell the patient. Doing so may not be helpful and could be very upsetting.

Some degree of amnesia is not usually a problem for patients unless they worry about it. However, they must also understand that lack of conscious memory does not prevent ruminations and nightmares involving these aspects of the trauma.

Chapter 53

"MARKEDLY DIMINISHED INTEREST
IN SIGNIFICANT ACTIVITIES"

One good possibility for diminished interest is that preoccupation with ruminations consumes time, energy, and focus of thought, and makes concentration difficult or impossible. However, learning to maintain concentration is essential to recovery. Therefore, patients must learn to return to activities of interest, and learn to fight off the intrusive ruminations by maintaining concentration. It helps to do something interesting, enjoyable, and satisfying, whether it is reading, working on a craft project, working on the car, playing tennis or golf, anything that requires complete concentration.

Someone who feels depressed does not feel like doing anything. They can learn, however, that pushing yourself to get started often helps. Once enjoying the activity, you are pleased that you gave yourself a push. Gradual success in returning to activities previously enjoyed gives the patient a boost in morale that helps overcome helplessness and discouragement. Learning that there are things you can do to feel better and to deal more effectively with problems is always encouraging. Positive feedback from staff is important in this process. The patient gets the feeling of returning to the former self, which elevates self-esteem and self-confidence. Pessimism can gradually be replaced by optimism.

Chapter 54

"FEELING OF DETACHMENT OR ESTRANGEMENT FROM OTHERS"

Group therapy is often the first step in dealing with this symptom. Group members relate to one another rather quickly, feeling they are with others who "were there," suffer from similar symptoms, and can therefore fully understand when they talk about a problem. Many individuals say it is the first time they have felt comfortable with others in a long while. Developing feelings of fellowship and trust with other group members is the start of friendships that are encouraged by staff. Group members who were formerly socially isolated are encouraged to meet one another socially for activities like going out to eat, going bowling or to a movie, to sports events or other activities. As social comfort increases, gradual return to previous social activities is encouraged. The group can also plan outings, picnics, or other activities to which they can invite family members and friends.

Chapter 55

"RESTRICTED RANGE OF AFFECT, E.G., UNABLE TO HAVE LOVING FEELINGS"

Group is where this sensitive subject can be talked about in the open. Group members can be very helpful to one another by understanding, and by discussing how they learned to deal with a particular problem.

Family and marital therapy is often important in helping these problems. Husband and wife can learn better communication and ways of helping one another. The patient usually welcomes this help because of guilt over behavior and isolation. A wife can learn, for example, that her husband's lack of interest and avoiding sex does not mean that he doesn't love her. Children can likewise learn that their father's isolation and anger at them does not mean he doesn't love them, and that he is trying to change. A spouse can learn to inform the patient when ruminations begin or when anger is starting to escalate. As families improve ability to communicate and deal with problems, the patient can gradually resume previous family and marital relationships.

Chapter 56

"SENSE OF A FORESHORTENED FUTURE, E.G., DOES NOT EXPECT TO HAVE A CAREER, MARRIAGE, OR CHILDREN, OR A LONG LIFE"

This symptom goes along with feelings of depression, and probably with the feeling of helplessness in dealing with all the problems related to PTSD. I therefore feel that a change in this symptom occurs only when the patient starts making progress in therapy, starts dealing with the problems, and is able to do more and more things that were formerly thought to be no longer possible. As improvement continues, the individual can gain optimism for the future, which effectively counters this symptom.

I have seen many patients successfully overcome this symptom after making adequate progress in treatment.

Chapter 57

"DIFFICULTY FALLING OR STAYING ASLEEP"

Many PTSD patients are tense and have trouble falling asleep at night, or are tense and watchful at night and can't fall asleep until they see the light of day. Schedules for sleep and meals become irregular, and patients often feel tired and lethargic.

I therefore explain that we have a *body clock*, that the body seems to function best on a regular schedule. If we eat at a certain time each day we will start getting hungry at that time and digestive juices will flow because our body is geared to that schedule. The same is true for sleep. If we keep changing the time we go to bed, and the time we get up, our body doesn't know when to sleep. When the time changes to daylight savings time, or when we cross time zones in a jet and have a new time for sleep and for meals, we don't feel good. That is called *jet lag*. If we go to bed and get up at various times, our bodies get confused, and you can't feel good when you have jet lag.

Therefore, one important way to feel better is to get on a regular schedule. A regular time to go to bed, a regular time to get up in the morning, and regular times for meals. One must stay on the new schedule for at least two weeks before the body starts adjusting to it, so trying it for a few days won't do much. Some people say they tried the change for two or three days, and it didn't work. The new schedule should allow for an adequate amount of sleep, usually eight hours, although some people need more, and some less. I reassure my patients that they will definitely feel better after they have stayed on the regular schedule every day for two or three weeks.

Keeping regular hours for sleep requires some education about normal sleep. Everyone is different, and some people fall asleep quickly and rarely awaken before morning. Others take longer to get to sleep and spend more time awake during the night. Such differences are normal and are not a problem unless you worry about not sleeping. We seem to get brainwashed by sleep aid commercials to believe it is problem if you are awake at night. If you lie awake and start worrying that you have a

156

problem and will be tired in the morning, then you have a problem and you will be tired in the morning. That keeps you tense, so it is more difficult to fall asleep, and you are not resting. However, I assure my patients that if they are resting and relaxing in bed during their scheduled bedtime hours, and don't worry about how long they remain awake, they will feel fine in the morning. If you are resting and relaxing in bed, your body will get the sleep it needs. We usually think we are awake much longer than we actually are during the night.

Resting and relaxing in bed does not mean reading, watching TV, or knitting, since these are activities. It means lying relaxed in bed with your eyes closed. If you are relaxed, chances of falling asleep improve. If a person likes to read before going to sleep at night, I tell them to do their reading before getting into bed. Bed is for sleep. Do not worry about how much time you are awake and how much time you are sleeping. If you must get up during the night to go to the bathroom or drink some water, go, but don't stay up. Go right back to bed. Just because you wake up, it doesn't mean you have to get up.

When people go to bed, they often find that their mind starts wandering, since there is no activity to maintain concentration like we have during the day. There is a tendency to review events of the day, review concerns or worries about the coming day or days, or any other concerns or worries that may come to mind. The result is insomnia and poor sleep for anyone. However, when one has PTSD, the wandering mind soon invites ruminations.

When I had the problem years ago, I realized after a time that maintaining concentration (while in bed) on something pleasant and relaxing could avoid or push away the disturbing ruminations. My favorite thought to concentrate on was lying on the beach, listening to the waves, and feeling the warmth of sun and sand. I clearly recall fighting hard to maintain that concentration, since the intrusive memories and ruminations kept trying to push in. With time I learned to maintain the concentration better and better, and it enabled more rest and sleep.

When I later learned progressive muscular relaxation, it was even more helpful. I therefore teach my patients this technique, and advise them to use it when they go to bed and whenever they are awake during the night. Since progressive muscular relaxation helps one relax and at the same time concentrate on breathing and muscle relaxation, it is an excellent way to avoid or fight off ruminations. The technique helps those who say they get too tense if they lie in bed awake during the night, and must get up. It helps them remain in bed and avoid body clock problems.

Some individuals have relaxation tapes from previous treatment that they prefer to progressive muscular relaxation. When their tapes both help relaxation and require concentration, I encourage them to use the tapes in the most helpful way. However, some have tapes for relaxation that provide only a sound, like the sound of waves on the beach. Although this type of sound is relaxing, it leaves the mind free to wander. When this is the case, I explain the reasons for endorsing progressive muscular relaxation.

Chapter 58

"IRRITABILITY OR OUTBURSTS OF ANGER"

This is often one of the most troublesome and frightening symptoms for PTSD patients, and it is dealt with frequently in all modalities of treatment. Patients want help with the problem because it interferes with their lives in so many ways. Loss of control is always frightening.

All symptoms, including this one, tend to grow in severity as daily time with ruminations increases. Consequently, one of the most important ways to reduce irritability and temper is to reduce time with ruminations. The patient should always be aware that there are things to be worked on that will help with this symptom or with any other symptom, so that helpless feelings in the face of symptoms are reduced.

Additional effort should be directed at learning to recognize the buildup of anger at an earlier stage. Initially, most patients complain that they suddenly become very angry and, "It comes from nowhere." However, anger usually builds up unrecognized over a period of time. The time may be long and related to the gradual buildup of pressure from spending time (patient unaware) with ruminations. The individual becomes aware of the anger only after an explosive outburst. When the pressure buildup gets high, temper outbursts are difficult to control. Since it is much easier to control before it gets too big, early recognition is important in the process of learning temper control. Even when the buildup of anger is more rapid, earlier awareness of the process can be learned in order to maintain control. Temper is never sudden, as it often appears to be.

Those with a greater problem of recognition can unknowingly be on the verge of a temper outburst and can't understand why others are reacting so strongly. They must therefore start noticing the reaction of others as one way of informing themselves about what is going on. Understanding family members and friends can also provide helpful information if they understand the problem, and if the patient asks them to help. This can be worked on in family therapy.

Once the anger is recognized, the individual can start making objective decisions about what to do. This enables clear thinking before an explosion occurs, rather than regrets and guilt after it happens. In this process, I usually ask patients about the reason for the common expression, "Count to ten," before losing your temper. Obviously, anything that can give you time to start thinking before you act can be helpful. Time to think gives you a choice of responses. Also, it is much easier to do something that prevents the explosion, rather than trying to undo the damage after the temper outburst. Therefore, if you feel close to losing your temper, it is easier to walk away and simmer down, rather than explode and deal afterwards with the consequences of the outburst. Consequences can include injuring others, injuring self, damaging property, and hurting the feelings of loved ones. Regaining a sense of control over this problem is very therapeutic.

Men often feel obliged to fight under many circumstances, since they can't allow themselves to be considered a coward. In group we talk about how grown men often behave like two kids with chips on their shoulders, daring the other to knock it off, step over a line, or whatever else means that they are obliged to fight. Does it mean you are a coward because you walk away from somebody who wants to fight? I often say in group, "If you feel obliged to fight with any stupid who wants to fight, you're as stupid as he is." Also, "You will stay very busy and have lots of bruises." Does it take good intelligence to fight? Obviously, it takes no intelligence at all to challenge or to start swinging. The intelligent person is smart enough to avoid fights. The only time you must fight is to defend yourself, which should happen very rarely if you are smart enough to avoid it.

If you fight and win, what do you win other than cuts and bruises? Fighting never changes anyone's mind or makes better friends. Rather, fighting makes enemies, with the loser often vowing to get even. Therefore, even if you win, you lose, particularly because fighting loses the opportunity for two people to work profitably together. An old Chinese proverb says, "He who strikes the first blow has lost the argument."

Many of the macho men have difficulty with the idea of walking away from any potential confrontation. They are often best helped in group therapy to learn that avoiding temper outbursts and loss of control has nothing to do with their manhood.

Another important way to help control temper and avoid fights is to try to understand where the other person is coming from. While I worked in the Veterans Administration Medical Center, this issue came up in group at times. How do you avoid a fight when somebody shouts at you angrily and says bad things? I would use my own example, where on occasion a hospitalized veteran would shout obscenities at me, and even threaten me. I would ask in group why I did not retaliate physically. Most group members would say that if it were them, they didn't see how a fight could be avoided. I can then explain that if something like this happened, I must understand that the individual was upset, and that physical response from me would be inappropriate, and would not help, but would instead aggravate the problem. Most group members could relate to this view, even though it would be difficult for them to do initially.

In treatment, patients are always given positive feedback for their effort to control this troublesome problem. The rewards of improved feelings of self-control are also stressed. Also important are frequent reminders that progress on these problems is gradual, and the efforts expended in this direction gradually bring increasing rewards. The rewards include such things as improved family relationships, improved social relationships, and improved employment adjustment. Because of the temper problem, many can't work at all. Therefore, improved ability to maintain employment can give the individual a big boost in self esteem. Reduced levels of anger also usually result in improvement of various physical and emotional problems.

Chapter 59

"DIFFICULTY CONCENTRATING"

When a PTSD patient is ruminating, or reliving a traumatic experience, it occupies full concentration even though the individual is not aware of what is going on. At such times, concentration on something else is not possible. Therefore, as with most other symptoms, reducing problems with concentration involves reducing time with ruminations.

Patients can learn to use this symptom to help themselves. We have already discussed the importance of learning to recognize ruminations earlier, preferably as soon as they start. Otherwise, the individual can spend long hours ruminating. I advise patients to try to read periodically to check on themselves. If they are unable to concentrate on reading, they are ruminating. Once they are aware of what is going on, they can quickly get to work to apply concentration to end the period of rumination. Trying to read periodically can therefore help the individual's efforts to reduce total time with ruminations, which in turn also helps the related memory problems.

In helping patients to learn to cope with this problem, I often use my personal experience. Upon returning to college, I found it very difficult to concentrate and study. This alarmed me because I wanted to go to medical school. I knew I could never make it if I didn't learn to concentrate, study, and get good grades. When I looked at a page and couldn't concentrate on it, I tried to fight it. That was difficult, and I would fight incessantly to get my concentration where I wanted it. I gradually became able to keep my concentration where I wanted it, even though I did not understand what was going on as well as I do now. The important thing is that my learning to get concentration where I wanted it was very therapeutic, and helped me a great deal. I learned in this way to fight off the intrusive ruminations and reduce total time with the problem. It took time, it was difficult, but my ability to accomplish this gradually improved.

I therefore encourage patients to use reading as one of the ways to fight off ruminations. There are many activities that enable people to apply concentration once they are aware of the need to do so. Once able to do this and reduce rumination time, individuals can improve family adjustment, social adjustment, and job adjustment. They can once again enjoy the many activities that inability to concentrate closed to them.

Chapter 60

"HYPERVIGILANCE"

This symptom can strongly affect the patient's entire life, including family relationships. As with other symptoms, reducing time with ruminations can reduce the severity of the problem. Reducing time with ruminations must always be a priority.

It is also possible for an individual to gradually ignore some of the alarm signals. For example, a man walking down the street with his wife can consciously fight off the temptation to look at people across the street by concentrating on his wife and his conversation with her. This is another example of the benefits of concentration. Here again, such efforts must be made over a period of time to enable gradual improvement.

One of the first steps in dealing with this symptom can be involvement in group therapy. Patients quickly become comfortable in group partly because the usual hypervigilance is absent. Group members can accompany one another to places that would usually cause hypervigilance. Their comfort with one another can help them work on overcoming the symptom. Family therapy can likewise help the problems at home.

As they continue to work on this problem it is possible for patients to gradually resume activities that were prevented by the symptom. Here again, progress improves family, social, and job adjustment.

Chapter 61

"EXAGGERATED STARTLE RESPONSE"

This symptom can cause annoyance and embarrassment. As with all symptoms, reducing time with ruminations helps reduce the problem. In addition, if the startle initiates rumination, this must be prevented or recognized and stopped as soon as possible.

One can also work on gradually reducing response to a given startle.[6] My personal examples of quick reaction to startles that prevent ruminations describe a way in which this can be accomplished. The intensity of reaction to a startle can gradually be reduced.[7] Most important in this process is the reduction of time with ruminations that can be triggered by the startle. With practice and effort, one can eliminate the problem of ruminations initiated by a particular startle.

Chapter 62

"PHYSIOLOGIC REACTIVITY UPON EXPOSURE TO EVENTS THAT SYMBOLIZE OR RESEMBLE AN ASPECT OF THE TRAUMATIC EVENT (E.G., A WOMAN WHO WAS RAPED IN AN ELEVATOR BREAKS OUT IN A SWEAT WHEN ENTERING ANY ELEVATOR)"

S ince physiologic reactivity is not usually anticipated, the problem is best dealt with like triggers for ruminations. One can learn to reduce or avoid exposure to events or locations that elicit the response to help the problem considerably.

As with all symptoms, reducing time with ruminations can reduce severity.

Chapter 63

DENIAL

Most of the considerations for dealing with the problem of denial have already been reviewed in Chapter 20. Feelings of stigma often lead to denial. We covered dealing with stigma in various ways, including showing patients the page on the diagnosis of PTSD from *DSM–III–R*. This helps them learn that they have an established diagnosis that is understandable and similar to the diagnosis of many other people. In addition, since PTSD can occur in almost anyone subjected to trauma, they need not feel that their problems make them different from or inferior to other people. Feeling ashamed of their symptoms (stigma) is therefore not appropriate.

We also reviewed how participation in group therapy helps everyone to recognize that they are not different, that others have similar symptoms and feelings, and admitting to these feelings and problems becomes less difficult. Group therapy is therefore an important way in which feelings of stigma can be reduced.

Another aspect of denial is the denial of ruminations, usually because people are not aware of them. Since they learn in treatment to become aware of ruminations and the consequences of spending time in this way, the spending of time reliving traumatic experiences is no longer denied.

Chapter 64

SUBSTANCE ABUSE

For those drug abusers who developed psychotic symptoms and were given the diagnosis of schizophrenia, making the correct diagnosis of PTSD is essential for appropriate treatment. These individuals are treated for dual diagnosis like everyone else with the combination of substance abuse and PTSD.

Early detection is important for children with this dual diagnosis, since physical or sexual abuse that causes PTSD often starts at a very early age. The symptoms are usually not recognized by children or the adults that care for them. Children usually deny the problems if asked. Substance abuse, which can start before age ten, is more often recognized than PTSD. It is vital that parents and other significant family members be involved in the treatment program if these problems are to be helped. Unfortunately, there are few programs for the treatment of dual diagnosis for children or adolescents. There is a great need for such programs to be developed.

Adults with dual diagnosis are often helped greatly by fellow group members who have had the problem, since the advice of a peer regarding this problem is so well accepted. Objective information about substance abuse can also be discussed in group therapy. Efforts in this direction are supported in individual and family therapy. Referral to Alcoholics Anonymous and Narcotics Anonymous are often made, since they are so helpful in overcoming abuse problems.

Most veterans I treated for PTSD had problems with alcohol at some time in the past.[8] Therefore, when someone entered the group who continued to have alcohol problems, they were helped and supported by peers who had been through it. Many individuals were able to stop drinking completely with this help from their friends in group. However, in some instances there were individuals who were simply not able to stop. They were encouraged to use an alcohol program and AA.

Chapter 65

DEPRESSION

Since those suffering from PTSD are usually depressed, treatment must generally include treatment for depression.

The symptom of ruminations contributes to feelings of helplessness and depression, so help with this symptom is important. Nightmares accompanied by behavior that awakens and frightens the family is another source of guilt and depression. Feelings of detachment are another symptom associated with guilt and depression. Irritability and temper are certainly symptoms that likewise cause guilt and depression. The symptom of guilt, including survivor guilt, contributes to the feelings of depression. Since each of these symptoms causes depression, it is apparent that treatment and improvement of individual symptoms is one way to relieve depression.

There are additional factors that contribute to depression, so help with these also afford relief of depression. The stigma and shame of having PTSD symptoms is often a factor. This problem is usually addressed in treatment. Guilt toward family for various symptoms and behaviors is dealt with in all therapy, particularly family therapy. The same is true for guilt about substance abuse.

Group therapy is always helpful in dealing with guilt. Others who have been through it are accepting and understanding of depression and crying. The individual finds acceptance and comfort, and it is possible to relate to others without the usual guilt and feelings of low self-esteem. Once comfortable with this group of people, with fewer feelings of guilt and low self-esteem, the patient can start relating to others in an improved way.

Feelings of helplessness and loss of hope also contribute to feelings of depression. As patients in treatment improve in their ability to control symptoms, these feelings diminish.

Antidepressants are consistently the most helpful medications for PTSD. When they are prescribed, they usually relieve depression along with other symptoms.

Chapter 66

CRYING

I know of no specific treatment for the symptom of crying, since it is part of the depression. However, in my experience the problem gradually diminishes with time as the individual improves and feels some degree of control over symptoms and problems, especially depression.

The atmosphere of understanding and acceptance in group is usually an important factor. Other group members can tell the individual that they too have or have had the problem, and there is no need to feel embarrassed about it while among understanding friends. They can also reassure the individual that with time in treatment the problem will gradually improve. With this help, patients gradually feel less embarrassed about crying.

The best help for the symptom of crying is treatment for depression, which was reviewed in the last chapter.

Chapter 67

ANXIETY, PANIC

Patients suffering from PTSD usually suffer from symptoms of anxiety, and may also have symptoms of panic. Anxiety and panic are usually the result of ruminations. Anxiety can increase as time with ruminations increases. These symptoms are therefore best treated by treating the PTSD and reducing time with ruminations.

As the patient improves with treatment and frequency and duration of ruminations decrease, symptoms of anxiety and panic also decrease. Medication can also help relieve the symptoms. When antidepressants do not offer sufficient relief, other medication may be added. This will be reviewed in Chapter 82.

Chapter 68

MOST COMFORTABLE WHEN ALONE

This symptom is related to many other symptoms, including triggers for ruminations, avoidance, hypervigilance, concern about control of temper, paranoid thinking, and the concern about being harmed by others. Relief from this symptom occurs only when some of these other problems are resolved.

Group therapy is often the first step in dealing with social discomfort, since most patients feel comfortable with others in the group fairly quickly. We already reviewed how group members can meet in pairs or small groups to go out to eat, to a movie, a sports event, to go shopping, etc. While out with the support of group members with whom they feel comfortable, individuals can start doing things they were not able to do previously. These individuals get positive feedback from staff and other group members for their progress in social comfort.

In both individual and group therapy, patients are encouraged to take small steps in becoming comfortable in more social situations. In social or work situations, they are advised to be cordial to others while keeping contact to a tolerable minimum. For example, one is advised to be as pleasant as possible, to say, "Good morning," to someone they are not comfortable with, and then move on to avoid undue discomfort. This could be a first step in getting along better with others.

As with other symptoms, this one also improves with the gradual reduction of time with ruminations and improvement in general condition.

Chapter 69

DISSOCIATIVE EXPERIENCES

Dissociative experiences are often cause for anxiety. The PTSD patient can also be alarmed and frightened by these experiences. Similar to a nightmare in some respects, little can be done in the way of control once the episode starts. I therefore focus on prevention.

As it applies to most symptoms, prevention is the most helpful thing to work on. Prevention includes reducing triggers, catching ruminations faster and applying concentration, regular schedule, regular exercise, having activities that provide enjoyment and the need to concentrate, relaxation exercises, and other therapeutic activities that have already been discussed. These efforts reduce all symptoms.

Since patients are usually concerned about what happened or what they may have done during the period of amnesia, explanation and reassurance helps those who may suddenly find themselves in a distant city, far away from home. First, they must understand that during the period in question, they have not done anything they don't usually do. I use the example of the average person with amnesia for a period of time while driving the highway. That person drove in the same way they always do, with the same care and attention to safety. They simply don't remember. In the same way, a PTSD patient did nothing unusual during their episode. They just don't remember. They therefore need not worry, as they tend to do, that they did something dreadful like injuring or killing somebody. Just because they don't remember does not mean that they did anything different than they usually do under similar circumstances. Repeated reassurance is usually necessary.

The patient with amnesia for behavior following a nightmare likewise needs an understanding of what happened, and reassurance that nothing dangerous or out of the ordinary happened in most instances.

Another concern is for the patient who has a medical condition that requires regular medical care and medication, such as diabetes or heart disease. If this individual sits in one place without moving for a day or more, serious medical consequences could result. Family members must therefore learn to help by understanding the problem so they can arouse the individual in a safe manner. Termination of the dissociative period enables the patient to resume appropriate medical care. The wearing of a medical alert pendant or bracelet could also be helpful.

I have known many PTSD patients who are troubled by dissociative periods. Over the years I have not run across an exception to what is described above. There have been only unusual instances in which an individual harmed another person or did anything different from what they usually do during the period of time they don't remember. For those rare instances where someone assaulted a spouse or damaged household objects after a nightmare, helping the problem is reviewed in Chapter 47 under nightmares.

Chapter 70

GUILT

There is always some guilt associated with the traumatic experience, and it tends to be related to lack of objectivity about what actually happened. The distortion of memory is always in the direction of guilt, of personal responsibility for what happened. Help must therefore involve improvement in objectivity.

Although objective explanations by the therapist can be helpful in this endeavor, group therapy appears to be most effective. The views of peers who have experienced similar trauma is strongly respected. Therefore, group discussion about an individual's experience and guilt is usually helpful. I will often share my own experience with unreasonable guilt when I feel it will contribute to the discussion.

My personal experience involved guilt that I was responsible for the death of many of my friends in combat. I would start thinking about each event and I would think of things I might have done differently that would have prevented the death. It took time for me to understand that hindsight is always better, and even when you do your best, bad things can happen. The bad things in combat were caused by enemy fire, and by the misfortunes of war. I had to keep reminding myself that I always did my best, and therefore objectively had no reason to feel guilty and responsible. I came to better appreciate how we are always smarter with hindsight.

In a PTSD group for combat veterans, an individual may be troubled by a traumatic event in which he shot a friend. The friend may have been dying and in pain from fatal injuries, but guilt and depression persist. Group members will reassure the individual that he did the right thing, even though it was done instantly almost in a reflex manner, that the victim was spared pain before certain death, and that they would have done the same thing themselves. Since group members become familiar with one another's problems, similar reassurance may be given in group at a later time if such help is warranted. Vietnam veterans often say, "We

175

had a contract," meaning that they were bound to kill a friend in order to protect him from a slow, painful death.

In a similar manner, this type of help could be offered in groups for PTSD that resulted from various causes. For example, in a PTSD group for rape victims, an individual could reveal guilt and depression over feelings that she provoked the rape in some way. Other group members would reassure her that she realistically did nothing provocative, and even if she had, it still does not justify rape. They would also relate to her feelings both during and after the incident. Peer questions can bring out facts about the individual's memories and behavior that need to be more objective. Self-blame and guilt are usually not objective, and can be most effectively dealt with in group therapy.

Survivor guilt is also best dealt with in group therapy. Here again, peers who have experienced similar trauma can relate to the individual with such guilt, and improve objectivity. They can remind individuals that they were not responsible for what happened, had no control over who lived and who died, that it was not something they could have realistically influenced in their particular situation. The forbidden wish for survival that increases survivor guilt is sometimes brought up in these discussions. Everyone learns that the wish for survival is universal, and that the wish realistically has nothing to do with who lives and who dies.

Chapter 71

PROBLEMS WITH MEMORY

As is true with most PTSD symptoms, memory problems are helped by reducing time with ruminations. Since frequent interruption of concentration and train of thought by ruminations appears to disrupt the memory process, reducing the frequency as well as the duration of ruminations should help.

We already reviewed the technique of catching ruminations instantly so that concentration can remain on the subject at hand. When this can be done consistently, memory problems are kept to a minimum. When a patient works on accomplishing this goal, it is done by gradually catching ruminations faster and more consistently. As the total time with each incident declines with appropriate effort, memory and other symptoms gradually improve.

Since the process of improvement takes time, patients must find ways to compensate for memory problems. They can start writing things down, and keep lists and reminders in a place where they check frequently. Remembering to look consistently is essential. A list does not help if you forget to look at it. An alarm clock can be set for meal time, medication time, and anything else that is important to remember.

When family members can help, it is important that they do so. They can remind the patient about medication, appointments, meal time, etc. Until the patient can remember more consistently, it may help for a family member to take responsibility for reminding the patient to take medication. This can't be done in a way that encourages irresponsibility, and the patient must always work toward responsible independence.

When a family member cannot remind the patient about appointments, I phone many PTSD patients on the morning of their appointment. I do this for those who often forget appointments, and who want me to help in this way. I continue to do so only as long as necessary, since I always encourage independence in all aspects of life.

Chapter 72

PHYSICAL AND MEDICAL PROBLEMS

Physical and medical problems are commonly associated with severe and long-term stress. Also, with PTSD there is usually reluctance to request appropriate medical evaluation and care. I therefore always inquire into medical history and physical health, and usually advise medical evaluation at the beginning of treatment. Many physical problems, such as thyroid disorder, can cause or aggravate symptoms of anxiety and depression. It is too easy to assume that all these symptoms are caused by a nervous disorder like PTSD and neglect to recommend physical evaluation. All medical problems should receive appropriate treatment. I always try to work closely with other medical specialists so efforts can be coordinated for maximum benefit to the patient. This is particularly important when more than one physician is prescribing medication, since the same medication could be ordered by two doctors, or the medications they prescribe could conflict with one another. I would check with a patient's cardiologist before prescribing antidepressant, for example, since some antidepressants are contraindicated with certain heart conditions. Dental consultation and treatment for bruxism and TMJ pain is often one of the medical needs.

Because patients are often reluctant to request needed medical care, one of the issues often addressed in therapy is the need to seek appropriate medical attention. Individuals are often encouraged to do so by their friends in group. Group members are very perceptive in picking up problems in one another. Someone in group might say to a friend, "You don't look good today," or, "You look pale today, what's the matter?" This would usually be followed by others encouraging the individual to seek appropriate medical attention.

The point is often made that good physical and mental health go together, that getting needed care for physical problems helps the nervous problems. Likewise, it works in the opposite direction. Calming the nervous problems reduces physical symptoms. For example, cardiologists have often encouraged me to use antidepressants, since high levels

178

of anxiety make cardiac treatment much more difficult. Group members often affirm this fact, stating that severity of physical symptoms and need for medication declined steadily with treatment for the PTSD.

Since ruminations are so stressful and upsetting, reducing time with ruminations effectively reduces physical stress on the body. Working on reducing time with ruminations is therefore one of the ways to relieve physical and medical symptoms. Remaining conscious of this relationship helps keep individuals motivated to work on their PTSD problems, as well as to pay appropriate attention to physical and medical needs.

Problems with anger and temper also come to be recognized as the PTSD symptom that creates a great deal of stress (that in turn aggravates physical symptoms). Working on these issues likewise comes to be recognized as important in reducing the physical symptoms. Poor control of anger greatly increases risk for the cardiac patient.

Chapter 73

PARANOID THINKING

Paranoid thinking and behavior is best dealt with in group, where group members become comfortable with one another. Under these circumstances, individuals can usually give up much of the guarding and defensiveness and deal with the subject more objectively. Paranoid problems are brought up and discussed at times because paranoid thinking and behavior causes many difficulties in daily life. Individuals admit to frustration when these feelings prevent them from accomplishing an objective, improving family or social relationships, or holding a job.

Learning to be more objective is always helpful. For example, stopping to think clearly before accusing a spouse of infidelity helps to avoid problems. In like manner, one can decide to meet another person for a social or business meeting, and to ignore the paranoid thoughts that would prevent or disrupt the meeting. The relative danger of going to a certain place, or meeting a specific individual, could also be more objectively evaluated after a little clear thinking. For those who feel some danger in leaving the safety of their home, group discussion can often help the individual to apply objective reasoning to deal with the strong emotions.

Since group members come to feel comfortable with one another, the paranoid individual can start going places that present difficulty with one or more friends from group. The group therapy atmosphere encourages members to help one another, and this is one of the ways in which they help each other. A gradual increase in previously prohibited activities becomes possible with the help of friends from group.

For those individuals who have family and marital problems resulting from paranoid thinking, family and marital therapy are indicated. A spouse can come to understand where the suspicions come from, and husband and wife can learn to work together to deal with it. For those with employment problems, group therapy and employment counseling can be helpful.

In many instances, medication can also help the paranoid problem if the patient is not too distrustful to take it.

Chapter 74

WORKAHOLIC TENDENCIES, OVERCOMPENSATION

When patients enter group therapy and admit to working two or more jobs, group members who are familiar with the problem explain it to them. They are advised to benefit from treatment so they can stop overworking and improve family relationships. They come to understand that reducing time with ruminations is an important way of reducing stress associated with overwork. They also learn that keeping regular hours and a sensible schedule reduces stress and helps them feel better. In addition, they learn that the stress of overwork can itself be a trigger for increased ruminations. Family and marital therapy may be helpful in reestablishing family relationships and resuming family activities.

The time that becomes available from reduced hours of work can be devoted to family, social, and recreational activities. Going places and participating in activities with other group members can help an individual resume doing things that they haven't done for some time.

Overcompensation that results from feelings of stigma are also often best helped in group. Feelings of self-consciousness because of being disabled are not infrequently the subject of discussion. I usually remind people that PTSD is *normal* because by definition these symptoms occur in most people exposed to extreme or life-threatening trauma. The fact that they have PTSD indicates they are normal and not abnormal. I say things like, "If somebody is shooting at you and you're not scared, you're not normal. Having strong emotions in response to trauma makes you normal."

When no level of achievement is good enough, it should always be even better; the individual feels driven, but always fails. The stress placed on self is an additional trigger for ruminations. The problem can be understood by other group members who have had the problem and learned how to ease up on themselves and obtain more satisfaction from their achievements. Once the problem is recognized, it can be gradually worked on and overcome.

Chapter 75

COURTING DANGER: THE ADRENALIN HIGH

The first step in dealing with this problem is recognition that it exists. This is often accepted best in group therapy when a peer who has had the problem points it out. In group it is less apt to be taken as criticism. Other group members then usually share in the perception and dimensions of the problem.

When individuals accept the fact that they court danger, the next step is learning to recognize when it occurs. Individuals must learn to monitor their reactions and behavior, so they recognize the urges and can therefore think clearly before they act. Each person must also learn to identify the ways in which they provoke risk and danger, since this understanding is needed in order to learn control.

The individual is motivated to learn control of this behavior after learning more about its consequences. Various consequences are enumerated by other group members. Physical injury is a common consequence, and many group members admit to numerous and often life-threatening injuries. Risking your life unnecessarily is recognized as behavior that requires serious control efforts.

Other consequences of this behavior include family, marital, and work adjustment problems. Family members are unable to understand, and work supervisors won't tolerate employees who endanger themselves and others. Family and marital therapy can help the identification and control of the problem, and family members can help the learning process of how risks and dangers are provoked, and what must be done.

Chapter 76

PROFOUND CHANGES

The first step in dealing with profound changes in personality and behavior is to establish the correct diagnosis. As already described, this can be difficult with PTSD because the individual is often not aware of the problem. One can be completely unaware of ruminations, so there may be no conscious connection between the past trauma and the related feelings and behavior. Partial or complete amnesia for the trauma can add to the problems of awareness and diagnosis.

For the child suffering from PTSD, making the diagnosis is even more difficult because of lack of awareness of a connection or conscious memory of the trauma, as above. In addition, parents are often unaware of the trauma to their child because the child is unable to talk about it or remember it. Reasons for the profound changes therefore remain a frustrating mystery unless an astute clinician is able to recognize the diagnosis.

Once the correct diagnosis is made, efforts toward treatment can begin. Treatment is also challenging because the patient is frequently difficult to deal with. Treatment is often rejected because of lack of conscious awareness of the trauma and the connection with symptoms, and the resulting refusal to admit to having a problem. Rejection may also occur because of irritability and anger over drawing attention to adverse symptoms, particularly in the presence of paranoid symptoms. A great deal of guilt regarding behavior may cause rejection of the diagnosis. The guilt can result from survival guilt, irritability and temper, abuse of substances, loss of job and earning ability, etc.

Motivating the patient toward treatment is therefore the first task. As already described, I often show patient and family a copy of the diagnosis from *DSM-III-R* so they understand that there is a valid reason for symptoms and problems. It is not something to be ashamed of, and treatment is available. This not only motivates the patient, but helps family to understand. When they understand, they can get help in family therapy to forgive the patient's behavior and assist in treatment. Family therapy is important in helping the patient toward once again becoming a functional family member. Desire to improve family relationships can also motivate the patient to get help.

When substance abuse is a symptom, it must be treated first. That is because use of a mind altering substance makes rational decisions and successful treatment impossible. Once this problem is under control, individual, group, and family therapy can proceed more successfully.

As symptoms gradually improve with treatment, the profound changes should also subside. One goal of treatment is to return the individual to the previous level of functioning.

Chapter 77

PTSD IN FAMILY MEMBERS

Family members are always affected and involved, and may themselves suffer from symptoms of PTSD. Family and marital therapy must therefore always be part of the treatment program.

Family members must first be helped to understand the problem, its cause, and the nature of symptoms. Reviewing and discussing the list of symptoms from *DSM-III-R* is often the first step. In the process, all family members must be helped to avoid directing blame and anger at the patient. All participants must learn to deal with the various individual symptoms. In addition, the many problems in marital and family relationships must also be addressed. For example, the symptom of irritability and temper leads to many family problems that require discussion since two or more family members can have a temper problem. The family is encouraged to work on the problems discussed during the following week, so they can work more effectively on things that are fresh on their minds.

The improvement that occurs gradually from increased understanding and control on the part of all family members leads to fewer symptoms and improved family relationships. Working together in the family has some similarities to members in group therapy helping one another.

Chapter 78

FAMILY AND MARITAL PROBLEMS

Family and marital therapy is essential in the treatment of PTSD, since the family is always impacted in many ways. Motivation for treatment must first be established, since the patient so often rejects any need for treatment because they say others have a problem, not them. Family members usually recognize the need for help, and try to convince the patient, who may take it as a form of criticism. As already described, discussing the cause and symptoms from the *DSM-III-R* list is a helpful first step. Once the patient is motivated to start treatment, the various problems can be dealt with.

Families are usually frightened and puzzled by the patient's behavior. They, as well as the patient, must be helped to understand the symptoms and their causes. Explanation and the answering of questions by the therapist is always in order. If substance abuse is one of the symptoms, it must be treated first, since therapy cannot proceed successfully when the patient continues to use a mind altering drug.

Family members can help with ruminations, reminding the patient when it occurs. They can also realize that the ruminating patient is not disinterested in them or rejecting them. They can help reduce time with ruminations, increasing family interaction. When family members understand and know what to do, nightmares can be less of a problem. The symptom of irritability and temper is often a major problem that must be worked on in family therapy, since it is so disrupting to family life. Family members can deal better with it when they understand the anger is not caused by their actions, but is a symptom of PTSD.

Detachment and loss of love feelings is another symptom that must usually be dealt with. Here again, family members are reassured when they understand the source of this changed behavior. However, it takes time to reestablish former relationships. Marital therapy is usually necessary to start a mending of the marriage, and hopefully a gradual return to the former marital relationship.

Treatment can often save a marriage, but sometimes a spouse will decide to leave and file for divorce despite treatment. Usually treatment enables the separation and divorce to be more amicable and reasonable, and free from anger and temper.

Chapter 79

MULTIPLE MARRIAGE AND DIVORCE

Marital discord, separation, and divorce are common, as already reviewed. Many PTSD patients have had up to five or more marriages and divorces.

The reasons for marital problems have been discussed, along with their treatment. It is not necessary to repeat them here. However, the therapist should be alert to the possible diagnosis of PTSD when the patient has a history of multiple marriages and divorces.

Chapter 80

STRONG REACTION TO ANGER AND VIOLENCE

Most PTSD patients react strongly to violence that is viewed directly, at home or on the street, or when it is viewed on a movie or TV screen. As previously described, such reactions can result in guilt or embarrassment. Parents who react too strongly to the squabbling of their children can be overly punitive and later feel guilty. The triggering of traumatic memories appears to be the major cause of the strong reactions.

Treatment for this problem therefore includes both the reduction of triggers and improvement of temper control. Both of these have been discussed.

Briefly, reducing triggers involves such things as avoiding TV shows and movies that portray violence of any kind. This often includes avoiding news broadcasts, since violence of some type is often discussed and shown in full color on TV. It also includes avoiding places where triggers may be encountered.

Various considerations involved in learning to control temper have also been discussed. Briefly, control is achieved by learning to defer any reaction until there has been time to think clearly about the situation so more objective decisions can be made. Reactions and responses are then consistent with what the individual prefers, and guilt over snap decisions and reactions is prevented.

Chapter 81

INTOLERANCE OF STRESS

In treatment, intolerance of stress is dealt with in various ways. When patients come under stress, they must learn to recognize it and be prepared to deal with increased ruminations. When one is prepared and ready, the start of a rumination will be more quickly detected, and concentration applied that will terminate the problem. I always encourage patients to avoid being caught unaware, or by surprise, since their response is apt to be slower, and they could be ruminating for some time before becoming aware of what is happening.

Reduction of stress should also become a priority. When one is aware of the increased problems caused by stress, one should try to find ways to keep it to a minimum. This could involve avoiding specific people, places, or situations, reducing workload, requesting a change of department at work, getting marital therapy when marital problems become stressful, or any reasonable measure that will reduce stress. If one is in a high stress line of work, some thought should be given to job change, even though it could mean some loss of income. Health needs must be given due importance and priority in life.

One stress already discussed is the tendency of many disabled people to have excessive expectation of themselves. They drive themselves to do more, which maintains stress. Another example is the individual who works two or more jobs as a way of keeping busy to reduce ruminations. Instead, the stress of a hectic schedule and insufficient sleep can increase ruminations.

Chapter 82

MEDICATION

MEDICAL CONSIDERATIONS

Before starting medication to relieve symptoms of PTSD,[9] medical information is necessary. Every patient should have a complete physical and medical examination, including indicated tests, such as EKGs, x-rays, and laboratory blood work. If the patient is on medication for heart or other conditions, the appropriate specialists must be consulted, as well as the internist who did the complete physical examination. There are many physical and medical conditions that cause emotional effects that could aggravate or even produce specific symptoms of PTSD. For example, an overactive thyroid can cause anxiety, agitation, restlessness, and irritability. Medication I prescribe could affect a medical condition adversely. In addition, interaction of two medications may cause problems.

Before starting medication,[10] I therefore consult physicians who are treating the individual. For example, if the patient was in treatment for a heart condition, I would discuss with the cardiologist any medication I want to start. If I proposed using an antidepressant, the cardiologist may suggest antidepressants to use or avoid, or suggest dose limits or adjustment of the dose of heart medicine. After that we would work together so as to avoid potential problems. In the same manner, if there was more than one medical specialist treating the patient, I would maintain communication with each of them. It makes sense for the various medical specialists to work together to make sure the patient gets the best treatment. Physical and emotional health go hand in hand.

ANTIDEPRESSANTS

Antidepressants are usually the most helpful medications for PTSD.[11] As already discussed, it is important to get the physical examination, EKG, and laboratory tests before prescribing them. There are some heart

193

conditions where they should not be used, as well as other medical conditions. If someone has a thyroid problem, they must be on the proper dose of thyroid medication before antidepressants can be started. If the patient takes other medication, it must not be one that interacts with antidepressants. Here again, consultation with the relevant specialist is important. It is important to warn all patients that mixing medication with alcohol or street drugs is a deadly combination that must be avoided. I will not prescribe for someone who feels that such drug use is a possibility.

The patient must also be educated about over the counter medicines that could interact with antidepressants. Decongestants, which are found in most cold remedies, can greatly alter the required dose of antidepressant, so the patient is strongly advised to check with the doctor about their use. Many patients can take their usual dose of decongestant along with the antidepressant without a problem, but should start on a small dose as a trial before increasing the amount. Some individuals can tolerate a smaller amount of decongestant than usual while taking antidepressant, but there are some who cannot tolerate even a small amount. Of course, dosages and medications should be altered only under the direct supervision of a physician.

Before starting antidepressants, I first explain to the patient that there are a large number of them, and if one was best for everybody there would only be one. Therefore, we may need to try more than one or two before finding the right one. Once we find the right antidepressant, then we must find the right dose. The proper dose is a highly individual matter, since one person may absorb the entire amount swallowed, while others absorb lesser amounts or even a small percentage. Some metabolize the medication quickly, while others metabolize it more slowly. With various individual differences like this, the proper dose for an individual can be large or small. If a person requires a larger dose than someone else, it does not mean they are more seriously ill, only that their body works differently. Antidepressants work best when the daily dose is taken regularly in order to maintain the therapeutic level in the body.

I then explain that we start on a small dose initially to be sure there are no reactions due to allergy or sensitivity of some kind. If there are no side effects or reactions, we increase the dose gradually until the desirable dose is found. Increasing the dose too rapidly can increase the possibility of side effects. Most people take a single dose at bedtime, one half to one hour before going to bed. Possible side effects of most antidepressants include drowsiness on arising in the morning, and for the first several days it may take a few hours before they feel fully awake. This morning drowsiness usually starts going away within a few days. If it lasts more than a week, I change to another antidepressant. I also warn patients about driving or using machinery when their reactions are slowed by medication, and often recommend that they first try a new medication or a higher dose on the weekend.

Another possible side effect is orthostatic hypotension. This is a feeling of lightheadedness or dizziness when arising quickly from bed or from a chair. If this occurs, the patient is advised to arise slowly and allow time to get steady before walking off. Starting to walk while still unsteady could result in a fall and injury. If this side effect persists for more than a week I change antidepressants.

Another possible side effect is constipation. If this occurs, I advise patients to drink plenty of water. If that does not solve the problem, I advise stool softeners to be used daily along with lots of water.

Another side effect I discuss with patients is dry mouth. Many medications cause dry mouth, but antidepressants can cause a particular problem in this respect. I advise patients to drink adequate fluids, to rinse their mouth out with water and swallow when necessary, use mints or chew gum if that provides relief. Most people get used to some amount of dry mouth after a time and don't consider it much of a problem. The dry mouth problem often improves with time, and many patients report that they no longer have any problem with it after several weeks.

I also discuss the fact that medication does not change the way you think, and a pill does not solve problems. Medication can help you feel better, sleep better, and calm down enough to deal more effectively with problems. When you are very upset it is difficult to think clearly and objectively to learn to cope with and solve problems in therapy. With medication you may therefore utilize therapy more effectively in the process of solving problems. The role of medication is to help the patient feel better while working more effectively to solve problems.

Before starting medication I also explain that almost everyone suffering from PTSD is depressed, and when one is depressed there is usually a change in the chemical balances in the nervous system. Antidepressants help to restore the normal chemical balances. However, after one has felt well for at least three months, we often try gradually reducing the dose. If the natural chemical balances have been restored by that time, nothing happens as the dose is gradually reduced. If at some point on the reduction schedule the patient notices a return of symptoms, it may mean that the balances have not returned entirely to normal, and that a higher dose may be needed for a time before the lowering of dose can resume. This explanation is particularly helpful to individuals with a concern over taking medication or becoming dependent on medication. I reassure patients that antidepressants are not addicting. You take them only for the time they are needed, and stopping them does not bring on withdrawal symptoms. However, abruptly stopping antidepressants can sometimes trigger the return of symptoms that existed beforehand, so gradual reduction is advised.

I also explain that the total dose taken daily is the important issue, since a regular daily dose maintains the proper therapeutic level in the body at all times. The importance of regular administration and not forgetting the regular dose is stressed, since skipping doses lowers the body level to below a therapeutic amount. The patient must therefore find ways of always remembering to take medication, or have a relative or friend help with the reminding. Since memory is often a problem for PTSD patients, I recommend family help in this matter since it is so important. Taking only one dose daily at bedtime can fit into a routine and make remembering to take it more likely. The single dose at bedtime also often helps sleep, and any drowsiness caused by this dose should be gone by morning.

I discuss with patients the fact that antidepressants are not fast acting, so regular daily dose is essential. It can take a week or more to get maximum benefit from a given dose, sometimes more than two weeks. Therefore, taking the regular dose is essential, even when the patient notices no improvement for a time. Antidepressants have a long half life and stay in the body for some time. That property lends itself to once daily dosage. After stopping antidepressants, most is out of the body after about two weeks.

Over the years I have had the most consistent success with two antidepressants, amytriptyline and imipramine. I usually start with one of them unless there are medical reasons that dictate otherwise. When the patient has GI spasm problems, these medications are often helpful because they slow GI activity. The antidepressants are also often helpful for headaches and neurologists use them to treat migraine. Cardiologists have often told me that emotional turmoil is more of a threat to the patient's life and health than any threat of cardiac complications from the antidepressants.

Before starting antidepressants I also explain to the patient that there are two classes of antidepressants, those that are stimulating and those that are sedative and help relaxation and sleep. For patients who are tired, lack energy and drive, and rest and sleep too much, I often recommend fluoxetine.[12] This antidepressant improves energy and reduces appetite for those concerned about excessive weight. This medication is taken in the morning, rather than at night, since it can keep one awake if taken late in the day. The starting dose is 10mg taken on arising or with breakfast, with gradual increase in dose to maximum benefit. I seldom give more than a total daily dose of 60mg, although at times 80mg is necessary. Side effects most common with fluoxetine are agitation and GI upsets, although I have seen very few of these problems. There are now newer antidepressants in the same general category as fluoxetine.

I usually start amytriptyline,[13] imipramine,[14] or most other antidepressants for outpatients at 25mg at bedtime for three nights. If there are no troublesome side effects, the dose is increased to 50mg at bedtime for three nights. The dose is raised gradually, using 50mg increases after a 100mg dose until full therapeutic effect is achieved. If for example the dose is increased from 200 to 250mg at bedtime and the patient reports no change or improvement from the higher amount, I suggest return to 200mg at bedtime as the regular dose. If this amount does not control symptoms adequately, I could suggest a change in antidepressants to try to achieve more therapeutic benefit. If the patient wishes to do so, I will start a 25mg dose of the new medication without changing the one already providing some benefit. If the new antidepressant does not cause unwanted side effects, the new one will be raised gradually as the old one is lowered. Finding the single antidepressant with the best therapeutic effects is my usual goal, although at times two antidepressants are combined if that is more helpful. One fairly common combination is fluoxetine in the morning and a small dose of trazodone at bedtime to help sleep. MAO inhibitors may be used at times with benefit.[15] Since antidepressants often relieve pain, they also help with painful conditions like arthritis that tend to keep people awake at night.

Sometimes the patient continues to have some troublesome symptoms despite a therapeutic dose of antidepressant. For example, if the patient has a good deal of anxiety or depression during the morning or afternoon, I may suggest shifting part of the bedtime dose to the earlier time to relieve symptoms. I explain that this does not represent a change in total daily dose, and taking 25 or 50mg once or twice earlier in the day is very helpful to some.

Another change of time of dose is sometimes helpful when the patient begins to have excessive morning drowsiness. I explain that some individuals have strong effects from the antidepressant in less than half an hour and must go to bed shortly after taking their dose. There are others who say they don't feel sleepy from medication for over an hour, and sometimes several hours. In those individuals, it can still have strong effects on arising. I therefore suggest that they try taking bedtime medication a half hour earlier each night. I keep moving it a half hour earlier until the patient reports getting sleepy from medication soon after going to bed. When that time is found, morning drowsiness is often no longer a problem. I have had patients who take their bedtime dose of antidepressant as early as 6:00 PM for best results.

I do not usually recommend antidepressants for PTSD patients without also recommending therapy, since medication can help make treatment more effective. However, antidepressants alone can help relieve symptoms, and some individuals will take medication but refuse treatment. I usually try to find one medication that will do the job, although there are times that other medication is needed in addition to the antidepressant. A discussion of various other medications used to treat PTSD follows.

CYPROHEPTADINE

Cyproheptadine is an antihistamine usually prescribed to treat allergy. However, it was found to relieve nightmares for some PTSD patients. Therefore, if the patient continues to be troubled by nightmares despite a therapeutic dose of antidepressant, I will recommend that this drug be added. It comes in 4mg tablets, and I suggest starting with one at bedtime. If that provides no benefit, I suggest two tablets at bedtime, and in some cases it takes three at bedtime to get the benefit. This drug is safe, not addicting, and it helps some patients get to sleep. If unpleasant side effects occur, the drug must be stopped. Some patients get partial relief from nightmares, and some get substantial relief. If there is no benefit from a 12mg dose, I discontinue the drug.

SEDATIVES (ANTI-ANXIETY AGENTS)

A troublesome degree of anxiety and agitation can persist despite a therapeutic dose of antidepressant. Sedative drugs may therefore be added when necessary. Since many sedative drugs can be habit forming or addicting, they present some special problems for those with long-term problems.

Many PTSD patients I have seen were prescribed benzodiazepines in the past and are quick to request them again. The benzodiazepines include such drugs as diazepam, alprazolam,[16] and lorazepam. They are all addicting, and stopping them abruptly may result in withdrawal effects that in some cases cause convulsions and death. Some patients take them when needed, but if taken regularly for more than two weeks and then stopped abruptly, withdrawal is possible. I have started seeing some PTSD patients who took benzodiazepines irregularly in a way that risked withdrawal, and I explain the risks to them and recommend a program of gradual withdrawal. With this I offer the benefit of antidepressants to help the distress, and possibly the use of a sedative that does not present the addictive risks to life and health. I feel that if at all possible, benzodiazepines should be avoided or stopped for PTSD patients. The some holds true for barbiturates and strong pain medications, which are also addicting and can have nasty or even fatal withdrawal symptoms.

There are not a large number of non-addicting sedatives. Antihistamines are used at times, but they tend to add to dry mouth and other side effects of antidepressants, and are therefore of limited usefulness. I have prescribed hydroxyzine with benefit for many patients. It is a very safe drug that can be used in doses up to several hundred mg per day if necessary in addition to an antidepressant. It has few side effects and is not addicting. An extra dose can be taken at times of high anxiety, and in some cases it also helps headaches and other pain. It is supplied in 25mg, 50mg, and 100mg tablets or capsules. I usually start a patient on 25mg once or twice per day, and gradually increase to find a therapeutic dose. As is true with all drugs, some provide benefit and some don't.

Buspirone is a newer anti-anxiety drug that deserves mention because it is not addicting and can also be used in addition to an antidepressant, and does not frequently cause side effects. While relieving anxiety, it also can have an antidepressant effect. Since PTSD patients so often suffer from depression, this can be an important part of the benefit from buspirone.

Buspirone is supplied in 5mg and 10mg tablets. I usually start the patient on 5mg once or twice daily, and if there are no side effects, gradually increase to get therapeutic results. If there has not been definite benefit on up to a total of 40mg per day, I stop the drug. Most individuals who will benefit notice improvement before they reach a total daily dose of 20mg.

ALPHA AND BETA BLOCKERS

These drugs deserve mention because they are also used along with the antidepressant at times. PTSD patients often startle easily or are hit repeatedly by anxiety during the day. These drugs reduce anxiety for many people, including anticipation anxiety.

After consulting the patient's internist, I first tried propranalol[17] in about 1982 with some success. It helped a very anxious and reactive PTSD patient relax. After that experience I consulted internists and cardiologists for individual patients, and they usually worked with me on choosing and adjusting the dose of medication. Alpha blockers were often considered safer and risked fewer side effects. Although I always handle the dose of antidepressant, I have rarely used alpha and beta blockers without consulting those with more experience in their use, particularly in the presence of cardiovascular problems.

MEDICATION COMPLIANCE

Medication is most helpful when taken regularly as directed. Since many PTSD patients have memory problems, they can forget to take their medication. They can often be helped by suggestions for a regular time each day to take medication, such as mealtime or bedtime. Some learn to set alarm clocks. Some are helped by putting their medicine for each day in a compartmental container so they always know what was already taken on that day. When suggestions like this are not successful, an understanding family member can help by reminding them. Some individuals prefer a family member to dole out each dose.

The macho individual who boasts, "I never take medicine, not even for a headache," presents another type of problem with medication compliance. The potential benefit of taking a given medication must be discussed. In some instances, fellow group members will succeed in encouraging someone to take the medication, enabling them to steadfastly improve.

The patient who is paranoid and distrustful usually refuses medication. I have had patients question me suspiciously about what is in the pill, or what they do to it in the pharmacy. These individuals will rarely take medication, even though at times they accept it and say they are taking it as directed.

Chapter 83

DURATION OF TREATMENT

The duration of treatment for posttraumatic stress disorder is highly variable. This is true for any category of illness, since every individual is different. Variable factors that influence the duration of treatment for PTSD will be discussed individually.

INDIVIDUAL VARIATION

Every individual is unique and different from others in almost all possible ways. The sum of their particular genetic makeup and life experiences makes for great differences in the way an individual responds to and is affected by a particular trauma. Likewise, there are huge differences in ability to respond to treatment and to deal with problems and solutions. If two people experience the same trauma, one could suffer minor PTSD symptoms or none at all, while the other could suffer severe symptoms. When two individuals suffer from similar symptoms, one could respond to treatment rapidly, while the other may require prolonged treatment.

In addition to the basic individual variation that is always present, there are other variables that could greatly influence the severity of symptoms resulting from trauma. These were enumerated in an early section of this book, and include factors like the existence of previous trauma (particularly a similar trauma) or the condition of the individual at the time of the trauma. Therefore, making general rules about the development of PTSD, the severity of symptoms, or the duration of treatment, are not possible. However, we can talk about averages regarding duration of treatment, recognizing that various factors strongly influence that duration.

In the past few years I have had medical reviewers and insurance companies inform me that treatment for PTSD is not necessary for more than six months, one year, or a similar arbitrary figure, and that the patient should be cured within that time. Further treatment that I recommend is not approved on this basis. I feel that such guidelines are arbitrary, and are certainly unfair to the patient. One need only look at the Veterans Administration. Some combat veterans have been treated for ten years or more, and they continue to have disturbing and disabling symptoms of PTSD despite the years of expert treatment, and I have known some of these individuals personally.

SEVERITY AND INTENSITY OF TRAUMA

The severity and intensity of trauma can influence the severity of symptoms and therefore the duration of treatment. There are obviously degrees of severity and intensity of trauma. Although trauma that results in PTSD usually involves the perception of threat to life, at least at some level, threat to life is overwhelmingly stronger in some types of trauma as compared to others. Brutalization by other human beings can intensify severity, as can physical injury. It is therefore possible for such factors to increase the duration of necessary treatment, either to a small degree, or to a great degree.

DURATION AND FREQUENCY OF TRAUMA

Some trauma that causes PTSD lasts less than one second, while other trauma goes on for some time and may be repetitive. The child who is frequently and repeatedly abused over a period of months or years is apt to have more severe symptoms and may require a longer duration of treatment. Another example is the ex-prisoner of war who was traumatized daily for one or several years, with many of those days including a number of separate and different traumas. Obviously, such individuals have severe symptoms and may require a longer duration of treatment, sometimes much longer than those with a single trauma.[18] This can be expected on average, although we must always keep in mind the great degree of individual variation.

REPEATED TRAUMA

We already reviewed the fact that previous trauma can sensitize one to subsequent trauma, which can then result in greater frequency, severity, and intensity of symptoms. This is particularly true when the subsequent trauma is similar to the original. One study found that the incidence of PTSD is much higher than average in combat veterans who were subjected to physical abuse as children. The impact on severity and intensity grows as the trauma is repeated. In combat, traumatic experiences are common and may occur daily.[19] For example, combat veterans who suffered PTSD in Vietnam and remained in service often had relatively more severe symptoms if they also saw combat in the Middle East war. The woman who was raped a second time probably also had a stronger reaction, or more severe symptoms. If it happened a third time, the symptoms are apt to be even more severe. Usually, greater severity and intensity of symptoms translates to a longer average duration of treatment.

TYPE AND FREQUENCY OF TREATMENT

The nature of treatment obviously has an influence on duration of treatment. The treatment must be appropriate, since at times inpatient treatment or a daily program may be indicated. Treatment is most effective when performed by competent, experienced staff. Outpatient treatment should be at least weekly and include the indicated modalities of treatment including individual, group, and family therapy, as well as medication. Therefore, if all indicated treatment is done, and done well, with appropriate frequency, the average duration of treatment will be shorter.

NUMBER AND TYPES OF TRIGGERS

A change in the number of triggers has a strong influence on the duration of treatment. If triggers are reduced, the frequency and duration of ruminations and other symptoms and emotional upsets are also reduced. The patient with fewer and less intense symptoms can work more effectively in treatment, reducing the average duration of treatment. On the other hand, when triggers increase, the frequency, intensity, and duration of ruminations and other symptoms and emotional upsets also increases. This obviously makes it more difficult for the patient to work effectively in treatment, and progress in treatment may be slow or the patient's condition may deteriorate. Some of the common triggers that slow treatment and increase intensity and duration of ruminations will be briefly reviewed.

Specific triggers are those that relate in some way to the trauma, directly triggering ruminations, or starting memories that in turn trigger ruminations. An example used earlier was a group of Vietnam veterans who were improving and doing generally better until Desert Shield/Desert Storm began. Pictures of troops and weapons were shown on TV many times daily for many months, it was usually on the radio, and people kept talking about it. These multiple daily triggers set everyone in the group back. There were more ruminations, more temper problems and other symptoms, and everyone's condition slipped backwards despite treatment. Most group members did not start improving again until some time after the war ended. Even though they slipped back, treatment helped to the extent that their condition would have been still worse without treatment. Using this example, if anyone had estimated duration of treatment for this group of veterans before that war started, the estimates would have required revision once the war began.[20]

In like manner, PTSD from any type of trauma can be made better or worse by a change in the number of specific triggers. An individual with PTSD from an auto accident can have increased symptoms after starting to spend time with a friend who can't stop talking about auto accidents. The same individual would also experience an increase in symptoms if required to spend time near the location of his or her accident. There can be many uncontrollable specific triggers for each individual that lengthen the duration of treatment in this way, even though patients are always encouraged in treatment to find better ways to reduce specific triggers.

In addition to specific triggers that are either direct or indirect reminders of the trauma, we have reviewed how stress is a non-specific trigger that also increases ruminations and other symptoms of PTSD. Stress from any source can therefore cause an increase in symptoms and a setback in the patient's condition. Severe stress will cause even more severe symptoms. Some common examples of stress include financial, business, job, and medical problems. Family and marital problems are also common stressors, since symptoms of PTSD such as irritability and temper frequently cause or aggravate these problems, and often lead to divorce. I have treated many patients who have trouble making progress in treatment because of the constant turmoil at home. When a spouse is willing to come in and participate in marital therapy, progress in treatment is more likely. When the spouse is unwilling to come in, the patient is more apt to remain upset with severe symptoms, and have difficulty making progress.

The stress of family and marital problems can therefore greatly lengthen the duration of treatment.

Another important and common category of stressors is physical illness and pain. Chronic physical illness is apt to cause high stress for many reasons. Some of these reasons are: physical discomfort, loss of job income, loss of family status, worries about procedures or surgery, worries about the condition worsening, the cost of care and medication, and complaints from family members and others. I stress chronic illness because it can have long term implications for the duration of treatment. Severe pain is another common stressor, particularly when the pain is chronic. As discussed earlier, severe pain tends to open the door to ruminations. For example, I have treated patients with chronic painful arthritis or herniated disc problems who had great difficulty making progress in treatment. Therefore, severe and chronic pain also greatly increases time with ruminations and greatly lengthens the duration of treatment.

FAMILY AND COMMUNITY SUPPORT

Family support is important if treatment is to be implemented away from the doctor's office and treatment setting. Patients usually spend most of their time at home, and the kinds of things happening at home can either shorten or lengthen the duration of treatment.

Some of the factors we already reviewed relate to the home atmosphere. A relaxing atmosphere is beneficial, while stress increases ruminations and other symptoms. An understanding spouse is helpful in many ways, and this understanding can be helped during family therapy. A spouse can learn to be understanding of irritability and temper, particularly when the patient can learn to say, "I'm sorry," afterwards. A spouse can help reduce time with ruminations by informing the patient that it is going on. A spouse can remind the patient to take medication or keep appointments. A spouse can refrain from being critical about the patient's inability to work. By setting an example, a spouse can encourage children to be understanding and helpful in similar ways and to maintain respect for the patient. These are but a few of the many ways that family support influences the duration of treatment.

People in the community likewise have an effect on the patient's rate of progress in treatment. When friends are accepting and understanding they can be very supportive. The broad community also has an influence, in terms of acceptance of this sort of disability, and the willingness of employers to offer jobs to former patients. A good example of poor community experience was suffered by many returning Vietnam veterans. After returning to this country by air, when leaving the plane, they were often cursed and spat upon by jeering crowds. When they returned home, friends and family in many instances refused to have anything to do with them, and they had to go elsewhere. They were often refused jobs, merely on the basis that they were veterans of an unpopular war. For those suffering from PTSD, these experiences were potent stressors that worsened their condition.[21] For a patient in treatment, experiences like this would certainly serve to lengthen the duration of treatment.

SECONDARY GAIN

Secondary gain is the term used to describe the problem of patients getting some type of profit or advantage from their illness. For this reason, they may resist getting well to some degree, usually without realizing it. This problem is of particular concern when patients were injured at work and became disabled and eligible for disability payments. It is likewise true in the Veterans Administration, where many veterans are treated for disabilities for which they get disability payments. There can also be advantages to having an illness or disability other than, or in addition to, monetary benefits. If a PTSD patient resists treatment and getting well even in part because of secondary gain, it is a factor that can influence the duration of therapy.

The possibility of secondary gain is one of the issues therapists must be aware of in the course of therapy. If it is present, it must be dealt with promptly so it does not impede treatment. Since patients are usually not consciously aware of the problem, they can easily become offended at what appears to be unfair critical accusations. These problems can be well handled in group therapy, since patients are apt to accept more criticism or advice from peers than from the professional therapist. Group members speak bluntly to one another at times. In a group atmosphere of compassion and understanding, there is great sensitivity to the feelings of others. I therefore prefer to deal with these problems in group therapy.

As with other factors that can influence the duration of therapy, secondary gain must be dealt with in order to keep the duration of therapy to a minimum.

SPECIFICS ON DURATION OF THERAPY

Prolonged posttraumatic stress disorder has usually been present for some years before the patient gets to therapy, often many years. Even when treatment is started sooner, the course of therapy is never brief. I have treated some individuals who were handling the problems well enough after about one year that they could terminate treatment and continue to work constructively on residual problems. There were even a few who terminated treatment in six or eight months, but I did not really agree that they were ready. A larger percentage of patients have been able to taper off and then terminate treatment after one to two years. The majority of patients I have known or treated took two years or more before being ready to taper off and terminate treatment. I feel that posttraumatic stress disorder is too overwhelming of one's life and personality to be treated successfully by brief treatment. As previously mentioned, I know many individuals suffering from severe symptoms that have had treatment for ten years or more, and who continue to suffer from serious PTSD symptoms. Although their treatment has enabled much improvement, the improvement is not sufficient to consider the termination of treatment.

In summary, therefore, I will say that the treatment of PTSD is never brief. I always hesitate to predict the duration of therapy, since there so many unpredictable factors that can slow progress, or even set the patient back for extended periods of time. Some of these factors are listed above. On average, I would predict that treatment will last at least two years, but recognize that there is apt to be a huge margin of error.

REFERENCES

1. Perconte ST: Stages of treatment in PTSD. *VA Practitioner 5:*47–57, 1988.
2. Rosenheim E, Elizur A: Group therapy for traumatic neuroses. *Current Psychiatric Therapies 17:*143–148, 1977.
3. Rahe RH: Acute versus chronic psychological reactions to combat. *Milit Med 153:*365–371, 1988.
4. Marshall JR: The treatment of night terrors associated with the posttraumatic syndrome. *Am J Psychiatry 132:*293–295, 1975.
5. Burstein A: Treatment of flashbacks by imipramine. *Psychosomatics 25:*683–687, 1984.
6. Fairbank JA, DeGood DE, Jenkins CW. Behavioral treatment of a persistent posttraumatic startle response. *J Behav Ther Exp Psychiatry 12:*321–324, 1981.
7. Ornitz EM, Pynoos RS: Startle modulation in children with posttraumatic stress disorder. *Am J Psychiatry 146:*866–870, 1989.
8. Jelinek JM, Williams T: Post traumatic stress disorder and substance abuse in Vietnam combat veterans: treatment problems, strategies and recommendations. *J Subst Abuse Treat 1:*87–97, 1984.
9. Davidson JRT: Pharmacotherapy of posttraumatic stress disorder. *Br J Psychiatry 160:*309–314, 1992.
10. Davidson JRT, Kudler HS, Smith RD: Assessment and pharmacotherapy of post traumatic stress disorder, in *Biological Assessment and Treatment of Post Traumatic Stress Disorder.* Edited by Giller EL. Washington, DC, American Psychiatric Press, 1990b, pp 203–232.
11. Embry CK, Callahan B: Effective pharmacotherapy for post-traumatic stress disorder. *VA Practitioner 5:*57–66, 1988.
12. Davidson JRT, Roth S, Newman E: Fluoxetine in posttraumatic stress disorder. *J Traumatic Stress 4:*419–423, 1991.
13. Davidson JRT, Kudler HS, Saunders WB, et al: Predicting response to amitriptyline in posttraumatic stress disorder. *Am J Psychiatry 150:*1024–1029, 1993.
14. Burstein A: Treatment of post-traumatic stress disorder with imipramine. *Psychosomatics 25:*681–687, 1982.
15. Frank JB, Kosten TR, Giller EL, et al: A randomized clinical trial of pnenelzine and imipramine for posttraumatic stress disorder. *Am J Psychiatry 145:*1289–1291, 1988.
16. Feighner JP, Aden GC, Fabre LF, et al: Comparison of alprazolam, imipramine and placebo in the treatment of depression. *JAMA 249:*3057–3064, 1983.

17. Kolb LC, Burris BC, Griffiths S: Propranolol and clonidine in the treatment of post traumatic stress disorders of war, in *Post Traumatic Stress Disorders: Psychological and Biological Sequelae.* Edited by van der Kolk BA. Washington, DC, American Psychiatric Press, 1984, pp 97–107.

18. Kluznik JC, Speed N, VanValkenburg C, Magraw R: Forty-year follow-up of United States prisoners of war. *Am J Psychiatry 143:*1443–1446, 1986.

19. Archibald HC, Tuddenham RD: Persistent stress reaction after combat: a 20 year follow-up. *Arch Gen Psychiatry 12:*475–481, 1965.

20. Kolb LC: Treatment of chronic post-traumatic stress disorder. *Current Psychiatric Therapies 23:*119–126, 1986.

21. Weiss DS, Marmar CR, Schlenger WE, Fairbank JA, Jordan BK, Hough RL, Kulka RA: The prevalence of lifetime and partial post-traumatic stress disorder in Vietnam theater veterans. *J Trauma Stress 5:*365–376, 1992.

SECTION V
ADDITIONAL CONSIDERATIONS

This section contains chapters on special considerations with combat veterans, legal considerations, and recommendations for dealing with disasters.

Chapter 84

SPECIAL CONSIDERATIONS WITH COMBAT VETERANS

The combat soldier faces an inner conflict between the strong fear of death or dismemberment and the strong need to preserve the closeness and respect of his comrades. Stresses in addition to prolonged enemy fire that may contribute to overwhelming the individual include fatigue from lack of rest and sleep, physical discomfort, hunger, and poor leadership.

Ernie Pyle was a famous war correspondent in Europe during much of World War II. He often accompanied combat troops and gave us many vivid and accurate descriptions of combat. He wrote:

A soldier who has been a long time in the line does have a "look" in his eyes that anyone who knows about it can discern. It's a look of dullness, eyes that look without seeing, eyes that see without conveying any image to the mind. It's a look that is the display room for what lies behind it — exhaustion, lack of sleep, tension for too long, weariness that is too great, fear beyond fear, misery to the point of numbness, a look of surpassing indifferences to anything anybody can do. It's a look I dread to see on men.

After observing the 1956 Arab-Israeli War, General S.L.A. Marshall said,

When fire sweeps the field, be it in Sinai, Pork Chop Hill or along the Normandy Coast, nothing keeps a man from running except a sense of honor, of bound obligation to people right around him, of fear of failure in their sight which might eternally disgrace him.

In his book, *The Red Badge of Courage,* Stephen Crane writes of a Civil War soldier:

There was a consciousness always of the presence of his comrades about him. He felt the subtle battle brotherhood, more potent even than the cause for which they were fighting. It was a mysterious fraternity born of the smoke and danger of death.

GENERAL

Those who suffer from PTSD following military combat[1] have some distinctive problems. Although it is possible to suffer from PTSD on the first day of combat, most veterans I have known and treated saw extended combat, more than a year, and even several years in more than one war. While in combat, one has traumatic life threatening experiences occurring daily for long periods of time, and possibly numerous very traumatic experiences in just one day. Surviving these conditions requires many changes in the way one thinks about and deals with daily problems and relationships. For example, we reviewed numbing, and also how individuals avoid getting close to any other person. Then when that person gets hurt or killed it is not so upsetting. However, this conditioning is hard to turn off, so that many years later the veteran is still numb and can't get close to others.

Those that remain in service after a war are usually troubled less by symptoms of PTSD than those that leave service. This appears to be true because they remain with people they feel can understand them. In addition, some PTSD symptoms like irritability and temper may be better tolerated in service because the individual appears to be "a tough soldier." While in service they can therefore continue to do things that would not be tolerated on a civilian job. Many of these individuals therefore start to suffer more severe symptoms after they retire from service.

After leaving the service, these veterans frequently choose to live in an area close to a familiar military post. There they will be close to other retirees who they feel will understand them and be tolerant of their special problems. However, living near a military post exposes them to military sights and sounds that trigger ruminations and increased symptoms.[2] They are often drawn to the very things that cause the worst problems.

When they apply for service connection at the nearest VA Medical Center or office, they must answer many questions and fill out forms regarding their traumatic experiences. Such triggers can be very upsetting. However, obtaining service connection can take two or more years. During that time the veteran may be asked to fill out more forms that are triggers, and answer more questions about their experiences. In addition, they may be called in periodically for review by a VA doctor who also requests details of the traumatic experiences.

EX-PRISONERS OF WAR

Those combat veterans who became prisoners of war suffered many additional traumatic experiences.[3] They were subjected as prisoners to brutalization and inhumane treatment daily, frequently for at least a year or two. When they finally arrived home, the reception was often not good. Many World War II veterans after returning home experienced the attitude that anyone who became a prisoner was someone who did not want to fight and do his part, but preferred to "sit out the war and take it easy." Some were unwelcome at home for this reason, and in some cases were shunned by friends and neighbors. As a group, therefore, ex-prisoners of war got in the habit of never talking about their military experience, and at times even denied that they had been in service. Over the years they built up resentment about the way they were treated after going through so much for their country. Because of this reluctance to talk about it, ex-prisoners of war did not for many years come to the VA for treatment. They were also more reluctant than average to get involved with treatment for PTSD.

VIETNAM VETERANS

As a group, these combat veterans had some very special problems. Many of them were patriotic and volunteered to join the service and serve their country. They were involved in a war that was difficult in many ways: the heat, not knowing who was the enemy, and seeing friends killed by children who had hidden weapons or explosives strapped to their bodies. At times they therefore had to kill children in self-defense. The combat was often frustrating. I have heard from a number of veterans the story that their unit was ordered to take a hill. After sustaining casualties to do so, they were ordered to withdraw, and the enemy reoccupied the hill. They were then ordered to take the hill again, and the same thing happened several times. They said it looked like the politicians were running the war, not the army. While in Vietnam they were aware of the distortions by the press and the unpopularity of the war. They resented that while they were risking their lives, there were demonstrators on the streets speaking against the war and against our servicemen who were in Vietnam.

The terrible reception these veterans received when they arrived home, with angry crowds cursing them and spitting on them was traumatic and is still resented by many. Among other things, they were called "baby killers" as one of the derogatory accusations. They were discriminated against in many ways, and usually found it difficult to find jobs. GI Bill benefits for training and education were not nearly as generous as for veterans of previous wars. Friends and family often rejected them, even wives.

Some healing of attitudes has gradually taken place in more recent years, and on average most Vietnam veterans have taken a responsible place in the community and workplace. Many Vietnam veterans now occupy leadership positions in local and national offices of all veteran organizations. The Vietnam Memorial apparently helped the healing process. Most of the veterans I treated who went to the Wall regretted going because it triggered lots of memories and ruminations, and they returned home very upset.

TEMPER

Most people suffering from PTSD have frightening problems with anger and temper. They say they get so angry so quickly that they fear hurting or even killing someone.

For the former combat veteran, these problems and concerns are apt to be greater. I have often heard their concern in comments like, "I was trained to kill, I can kill someone with my bare hands. If I lost my temper I could kill someone before I knew what was happening." This makes the fear of losing control of temper even greater than average. Their concern is heightened by past fights or incidents they did not even remember afterwards. This prompts statements like, "I could kill somebody and not even remember doing it." These concerns are frightening to the individual, since there are various aspects of military training and experience that could implement a lethal physical attack on others. This includes such things as planning and execution of the attack, good marksmanship, and proficiency in the martial arts.

Therefore, the concerns about temper and loss of control tend to be greater than average for the veteran group. Some individuals are quite frightened by what they might do. Despite the concerns and fears about losing control, and potential consequences, the concerns rarely materialize. I never met one combat veteran with such concerns that had seriously harmed someone.

THE ADRENALIN HIGH

The *adrenalin high* is the elated feeling that accompanies fear and the release of adrenalin. That is essentially the pleasure of riding a roller coaster or jumping out of an airplane with a parachute. The fear causes release of adrenalin that can bring on pleasant feelings of elation. This is not a universal phenomenon. Many children don't like roller coasters, for example, because they are unpleasantly frightening. Likewise, many servicemen in combat never experience the adrenalin high.

Since combat soldiers may be exposed to frightening situations many times daily, after a time some of them come to relish and enjoy the adrenalin high. They now describe it as an "adrenalin rush" during which they feel very good, very alert so they don't miss anything, and they have amazing strength. They cite examples of individuals lifting up a car to free someone, a lifting of weight that could never be accomplished under normal circumstances. It is such a good feeling that they keep wanting to get it back. They say, "If you could bottle it, it would put all the other drugs out of business." I have heard things like this from combat veterans fairly often, but never from someone with PTSD from another cause (however, I'm sure there are non-veterans with the problem).

Some of these individuals who remained in service after a war kept requesting the most dangerous assignments. For those who left service, they likewise often went into areas of work or recreation that would reproduce the adrenalin high. One of the problems for these veterans was the attraction to get into fights that would give them the high and the strength to win. They feel they can't lose. However, getting into fights also gets them into the fear of harming or killing someone, so they know they must learn to resist all temptations to fight. Nevertheless, they are apt to talk with nostalgia about that good feeling when you can do anything because you have superhuman strength.

EFFECTS ON THE FAMILY

Everyone in military service is conditioned to strict discipline. When a sergeant orders a soldier to do something, it is to be done immediately and without question. Obeying orders is very much a part of military life.

This conditioning is apt to be brought home by the serviceman or discharged veteran in various ways. Most troublesome is a tendency to treat wife and children somewhat like privates, barking orders and getting extremely angry when those orders are not promptly obeyed.

When the serviceman or veteran also has PTSD, this problem is compounded by the symptom of irritability and temper. The anger can be excessive, for example, when one of the children doesn't obey promptly. Then the shouting and punishments may also become excessive. This is one of the important problems that can lead to divorce. I must admit to some problems of this type when I and my children were younger. Fortunately, I gradually changed with the help of a patient and understanding wife, and the children were able to forgive my previous excesses in discipline.

I have heard many veterans during PTSD groups agree on the fact that most of them alienated their children because of this problem and could never be close to them. After the children have grown it is too late, and they can never be close to their grown children. They have deep regrets now, but at the time felt that they were justified in what they said and did. Those with younger children still have some opportunity to change things. We talk about how they must learn to control temper, to stop treating their children like privates, and must learn to tell their children they are sorry if they lose their temper. Changes like this take time and effort, but can be very rewarding.

STAYING ON GUARD

Another habit one can get into in military combat is the habit of staying on guard and alert for danger twenty-four hours a day. Your life and the life of your comrades can depend on it. Therefore, one is watching for every movement and every possible sign of danger constantly. Sleep is apt to be light, with one becoming instantly awake and alert at the slightest sound. After combat, this habit or conditioning persists, won't turn off, and can lead to various problems. Although the symptom of hypervigilance can result from trauma of all types, the problems related to this symptom are apt to be more severe in combat veterans.

One of the problems already reviewed is constant watching and scanning, which is a trigger for traumatic combat memories and experiences. For example, the individual who is driving along the highway looking for possible sites for hiding enemy troops, or for possible tank maneuver areas, is triggering ruminations and increased symptoms. I will not give other examples here, but merely make the point that this type of behavior leads to more severe symptoms of PTSD.

A related problem is the tendency for some of these combat veterans to go on guard at sundown when it starts to get dark. They can become more alert at this time, listening for any sound and watching for any movement. Some are unable to sleep at night because of this need to be on guard, and can relax and fall asleep only after the sun comes up in the morning. This activity likewise triggers ruminations and more severe symptoms.

SUDDEN AGGRESSIVE BEHAVIOR

There are two situations in which combat veterans can suddenly become aggressive and even potentially dangerous. One is following a nightmare when the individual is still not fully awake. I have treated many veterans who were hitting, punching, or strangling their wives because they were continuing and acting out the nightmare. Their wives were enemy soldiers until they became fully awake, at which time all such activity stopped. Many refused to sleep in the same room with their wives after they hurt their wives, for fear they might harm them again even more severely. Some of these veterans get out of bed while continuing the nightmare. I gave one example of a veteran swinging a baseball bat and smashing furniture and lamps that were enemy soldiers until he was fully awake. Fortunately, his wife was able to keep a safe distance away while trying to awaken him. I have never known of a serious or fatal injury during one of these episodes.

The other potentially dangerous situation is a flashback in which an individual is suddenly back in a combat situation, but it happens during the day. If it happens on the street, the veteran can suddenly start attacking people on the street who are seen as enemy soldiers. This experience is similar to the behavior associated with a nightmare described above, and the episode terminates only when the veteran is fully awake and fully conscious of his surroundings.

Flashbacks as described here are apparently rare. Of the hundreds of veterans I have talked to who have PTSD, I have never met one who had this type of experience. Although it is possible for individuals with PTSD from trauma other than military combat to have these problems, I think they would be less dramatic. However, we can't say it is not possible, even though quite rare.

ANNIVERSARY REACTIONS

Anniversary reactions are common with PTSD from any trauma. The anniversary reactions for combat veterans are unique in some ways. There are often such reactions to the date someone was severely injured, the day their plane was shot down, the date of becoming a POW, or various special combat events. In addition, holidays are often a time for anniversary reactions. For those that were in combat and away from home at holiday time, the holidays can be special times to bring on memories and ruminations. In my own case, I spent one Christmas in combat. Although I never had serious anniversary reactions at that time of year, my memory of that time in combat is more clear than the memory of most other combat time. I also can't help recalling it without some emotion, even though such emotions have not been strong for many years.

To use examples of anniversary reactions, while in treatment for PTSD I have fairly often heard someone say, "I felt bad the past week or two, I just realized that last week was the date I was wounded." It could be another type of combat event. At such times, the individual may fail to recognize that the reason for not feeling well is because of spending more time with ruminations.

LOVING GUNS

Combat veterans usually carried guns while in combat. A personal weapon, or gun, was their major personal protection for times when their lives were threatened. They slept with one and ate with one since it had to be instantly ready day or night without warning. Many combat veterans became familiar with the use of a number of guns and weapons they could use should the need arise. Without a gun in combat, a soldier would be extremely vulnerable, since guns ready for instant use were vital to survival. Going anywhere without a gun would be no more considered than going naked. Without a gun handy, therefore, one would feel vulnerable, very uncomfortable, and out of place. Suddenly not having a gun would cause great anxiety and discomfort.

After returning home from a war in which a gun was carried or within reach day and night for months or years, veterans find themselves feeling very uncomfortable and vulnerable without a gun. The feeling is so strong that many go out and buy guns, and some can't leave the house without carrying a loaded gun. I have known many veterans who admit to carrying a concealed gun wherever they went for a number of years before they were able to go out without one. A few have never been able to give up this practice, even though they know it is against the law and they could be fined and suffer additional consequences. The need to have that gun is too strong. Despite the fact that so many combat veterans have done this for reasons relating to personal comfort and peace of mind, rather than any actual threat, it is very rare that one is used in anger. I have never run across such an incident. This is also true for the many combat veterans who keep guns at home, and those who sleep with a loaded gun under their pillow or within easy reach.

In my own case, I woke up in an army hospital after being injured, and spent close to two years in the hospital. I can recall very strong feelings of discomfort without my rifle within reach. These feelings remained strong for many months, but of course I could never talk about it. I recall trying to buy a pistol from another injured veteran who had one hidden in his personal bag. Neither of us were able to walk or leave the bed, and in the hospital we had no realistic need for a gun.

Some combat veterans simply love guns. They collect them, look at them and stroke them fondly, heft them, aim them, and clean and polish them. Some enjoy target practice, and take pride in their marksmanship. They look at and talk about guns with fellow veterans who have the same interest. I have heard these veterans say things like, "A good gun is like a good woman, you feel it, stroke it, you feel good when it is near, makes you feel good."

THE HOME FORTRESS

Some combat veterans who suffer from PTSD have very severe symptoms of avoidance and hypervigilance. They may feel very uncomfortable any time another human being comes within several feet of them. Some of these individuals try to spend time alone in the deep woods, or move into the country where they will rarely see another person.

In a few instances, hypervigilance is so severe that the veteran may start building a fortress, using military knowledge learned in combat. It can be done to various degrees. He may go to the extreme of establishing a perimeter, stringing barbed wire, have vision in all directions so nobody can sneak up, and establish lines or fields of fire. He may have several guns and a stockpile of ammunition. Although this is a rare but potentially dangerous situation, I am again not aware of any instances in which someone was injured under these circumstances.

IMPLICATIONS FOR TREATMENT

Treating a group of combat veterans for PTSD, rather than mixing them with PTSD patients who suffered other types of trauma, offers the advantage of their sharing and understanding the special considerations outlined above. However, since the veterans feel that their problems and symptoms are different, it can make them feel different from other people in the community. With this, they can also feel that others in the community don't understand them, and perhaps discriminate against them. That would go along with paranoid feelings, and work against treatment and readjustment to the community.

Mixing patients who suffered various types of trauma in a PTSD group has the advantage of helping them focus on symptoms of PTSD that they all share to various degrees. This reduces the tendency to focus on differences and uniqueness. It would therefore help veterans readjust to the general community and reduce the described problems if they were treated in mixed groups.

The process of forming groups for group therapy has always involved the decision as to whether therapy goes better with patients of similar age, sex, diagnosis, etc., or with a mixed group of patients. In general, I feel there are usually more advantages to a mixed group. Working for the Veterans Administration kept me treating exclusively combat veterans in the PTSD groups, and I have no experience treating them along with those who suffered other types of trauma. However, I still feel that mixed groups could offer some advantages.

Chapter 85

LEGAL CONSIDERATIONS

GENERAL

There are two legal situations in which the diagnosis of PTSD can become an issue. One is in workmans' compensation proceedings, and the other is in a court of law.[4] In a court of law, one can sue for either physical or emotional injury, or for both at the same time. Also in a court of law, however, the diagnosis of PTSD may be used as a defense against prosecution for a criminal act.

WORKMAN'S COMPENSATION

In a workmans' compensation case,[5] relationship of symptoms to the injury must be clearly established. The exact nature of the injury or trauma, how it was responsible for symptoms of PTSD, and the severity of physical injury, are all relevant. It must also be clear that the patient has legitimate symptoms and is not malingering.

Everyone who suffers trauma does not develop PTSD. Therefore, to establish that symptoms of PTSD are related to the trauma, the symptoms cannot have existed beforehand. Information about previous symptoms must be obtained from the patient, from family, friends or employers, and from past medical records. In addition, specific symptoms of PTSD can relate to the trauma. For example, an employee who was injured by a falling heavy metal object could have nightmares of again being pinned under a heavy metal object. The clinical experience of the examiner in evaluating PTSD is also important, since evaluation by someone experienced produces findings that have objective validity. Although physical injury makes the development of PTSD more likely, the severity of physical injury is not a relevant issue. The severity of PTSD has no direct relationship to the severity of physical injury. It is quite possible to develop PTSD without physical injury or trauma. This must be

223

mentioned, since it is too easy to assume that the more serious the physical injury, the more severe the symptoms of PTSD.

Compensation for a physical disability cannot be related to disability from PTSD, since they are separate issues. Fault is not an issue with workmans' compensation. However, duration of disability and duration of necessary treatment are important issues, since the bills for treatment must be paid. As already discussed, it is difficult to predict duration (see Chap. 83). However, the examiner can be expected to estimate a range of time over which there will be need for treatment for PTSD.

SUIT FOR PERSONAL INJURY

Suit for personal injury in a court of law involves a suit for damages by the injured person against the individual or corporation held responsible. Who is at fault and who is responsible are important issues in this legal situation. In most other respects, however, the issues are similar to those in a workmans' compensation hearing. It must be evident that the patient who suffers from PTSD is not malingering.[6] Relationship of symptoms to the injury must be clear. This relationship is verified by past patient history, and examination by an experienced and qualified expert who is called an expert witness, and who confirms that the patient suffers from PTSD related to the trauma in question. Issues of physical injury and PTSD must be kept separate. It is always important to explain why the severity of physical injury has no direct relationship to the severity of PTSD symptoms.

In the adversarial court situation, an expert witness may be challenged. I don't see that as a problem, since the qualified therapist has a great deal of objective information. The monetary value of pain and suffering is not an issue for the therapist. However, the therapist must here again be able to estimate a range of time during which the patient will need treatment, since the duration of disability and cost of treatment are relevant issues.

DEFENSE AGAINST CRIMINAL PROSECUTION

For a number of years the diagnosis of PTSD has been used as a defense in criminal cases. In my opinion, PTSD is rarely the cause of criminal behavior, although there are two situations where it is possible. Before discussing them, a few things must be said about the use of PTSD as a defense in a criminal trial.

As with a suit for injury, it is first necessary to establish that the defendant indeed suffers from PTSD. This is best done by the expert witness who has experience with the evaluation and treatment of PTSD. The trauma that caused the PTSD is relevant only in special circumstances that will be discussed. Whether or not a physical injury was associated with the trauma is likewise not relevant.

In order to be considered not legally responsible for a criminal act, the individual must have a mental illness that prevents him from understanding the nature of his act, or he is subject to irresistible impulse.[7] Legally, some form of either of these two problems can result in the defendant not being held criminally responsible for a crime. The individual will be sent to a mental hospital for treatment rather than to prison.

In general I regard those suffering from PTSD as people who know the difference between right and wrong, and who are able to control their behavior sufficiently that they can avoid criminal acts. Therefore, if the individual who suffers from PTSD committed a crime while under the influence of alcohol or drugs, it merits legal treatment no different from the person who does not suffer from PTSD. Although problems with temper control are often a symptom of PTSD, it is rare that temper is lost to the degree that a criminal act occurs.

The first type of exception is the blind rage that occasionally occurs with PTSD. There are times that the individual builds to a rage and "snaps." Under these conditions, the individual can become very violent and have no memory of the event.[8] Someone could be seriously injured or even killed when this happens.

As already indicated, this occurs very rarely with PTSD. I have talked to veterans who had fights while drinking that they could not remember afterwards. I doubt that is different from someone without PTSD who has been drinking. Although I have heard quite a few such stories from PTSD patients, there was not one instance in which a serious injury resulted from the fight that was not remembered. If a PTSD patient used this as a defense against murder, for example, I would want to be sure there was no premeditation involved, and that the individual had previous episodes of uncontrolled violence with amnesia, and the previous episodes are clearly documented. If this was clearly the case, I might be willing to say that the irresistible impulse test was met.

The other special symptom described is dissociation related to a period following a nightmare, or the flashback that occurs during the day. In either situation, the individual is reliving a traumatic episode from the past. I have read about this happening only in combat veterans, although I think it is possible with PTSD from any type of trauma. I have read about occasions where a veteran suddenly started attacking people on the street whom he saw as enemy soldiers at the time. I feel that the flashback in which this occurs is quite rare, since I have not seen good documentation in the literature and never knew a single patient who had such an episode.

I have heard numerous stories of patients who hit or tried to strangle their wives before they awakened fully from a nightmare. Here again I have never heard of a serious or fatal injury under these circumstances. If a fatality occurred as a result of such a nightmare related episode, I would consider that the patient suffered from a mental illness that prevented him from understanding the nature of his act. Before doing so, I would want to be certain that the individual had similar episodes in the past that were well documented.

Since these are the only two rare circumstances under which I would not consider a PTSD patient legally responsible for a crime, I would like to stress a few important points. First, such instances are quite rare. Also, in both situations, the problem is sudden, unpredictable, with unexpected anger resulting in explosive violent behavior. This is important because I do not consider PTSD to be a valid defense where there is premeditation and planning, or with non-violent behavior, such as robbery or the sexual abuse of a child. I would also not consider rape to be related to PTSD, since rape is not the described explosive type of violence. Rape also involves a sequence of behaviors that require control and planning.

As described, the evidence that an individual suffers from PTSD is an objective finding when the examiner is a therapist with experience in the evaluation and treatment of this disorder.[9] However, the diagnosis at times depends heavily on information from a patient who may have ulterior motives. Consequently, there is always a search for even more objective measures. Such measures[10] have been worked on for a number of years, and could be desirable in a legal situation.

The first work of this kind I became aware of was done in a Veterans Administration Hospital a number of years ago. Sensors were attached to Vietnam veterans to measure things like heart rate, respiration rate, blood pressure, muscle tension, and skin moisture. Those veterans who suffered from PTSD had very different readings than fellow combat veterans who did not have PTSD when they all watched videotapes of military combat, or when combat sounds were played. More recently, similar physiologic reactions were measured on patients with PTSD from various causes when they were read a sequence relevant to their particular trauma.[11] Since the physiologic reactions of the PTSD patients are distinct when they are exposed to triggers for their trauma, I suspect that a standardized test will be developed over the next several years.[12] This would be objective information that may be used in court, or any other time the diagnosis of PTSD needs to be confirmed by an objective test.

Chapter 86

RECOMMENDATIONS FOR DEALING
WITH DISASTERS

Disasters[13] occur in small, medium, and large sizes. Each type requires a different level of response. Small ones involve one or just a few victims. Examples of small disasters include auto accidents that injure the occupants of one or two vehicles, fire in a house that injures one or more family members, a family fight in which one or more people are injured, or a holdup in a small store resulting in one or more injuries. Small disasters may involve a few onlookers in the immediate vicinity, plus police, firemen, medical emergency crews, and medical personnel in the hospital.

Medium disasters involve more victims and onlookers, and require a greater variety of services and more personnel than small ones. Examples would include wild shooting by a gunman in a restaurant that injures and kills a number of people and traumatizes many others who were not physically injured, a tornado or flood that injures a number of people and traumatizes many others, or an explosion in a small factory that injures a number of individuals and traumatizes all employees.

Large disasters involve large numbers of people. Some victims may be injured or killed, but everyone is traumatized to some degree. Examples would be an earthquake that damages a region or an entire city, or a hurricane that damages an entire region. We experienced both of these disasters in the recent past, and many victims continue to suffer the consequences. Large or major disasters therefore require response not only at the local level, but response at the state and national levels.

I think it would be most helpful to examine one example of each size of disaster and discuss the various considerations involved. Each size of disaster shares victims and witnesses who are traumatized, and the usual emergency units. The larger the disaster, the greater the variety and numbers of involved personnel, departments, agencies, and organizations.

In this review I will refer often to the section on prevention of PTSD (Chapter 40).

A SMALL DISASTER

As an example of a small disaster,[14] I will discuss the collision of two automobiles, with serious injuries to one occupant in each auto. Police were first on the scene. They called for an emergency medical unit, the fire department to deal with the threat of leaking gasoline, and tow trucks to remove the vehicles after the occupants have been cared for. Four people who happened to be walking nearby stayed to watch.

I will first talk about the occupants of both automobiles. There were a total of five occupants, and two were seriously injured. The other three had cuts and bruises. Primary prevention of PTSD for all five people would have included some previous training in dealing with medical emergencies so they could help themselves and one another and know what to do and what not to do. They would know what type of help to expect, and how to cooperate with such help. What happens would then be less frightening, and they could reassure one another. Those who were seriously injured need most reassurance, since they are also more at risk for developing PTSD.

Police, firemen, and emergency medical personnel are regularly called upon in emergencies to assist people who are often seriously injured and bleeding. Hopefully, they all have training that provides primary prevention for PTSD, plus adequate opportunities for debriefing and group discussions. Such programs are becoming more widely available.

Four witnesses on the street, and two tow truck drivers have been traumatized by observing the serious injuries. Hopefully they have also had the benefit of primary prevention. However, it is unlikely that secondary prevention opportunities will be available to them. That is another area of concern that should be addressed.

When the accident victims are brought to a hospital, they are cared for by doctors, nurses, and other medical personnel who frequently care for seriously injured and dying people. Not many hospitals currently have primary and secondary prevention programs for medical personnel, but I hope that will change. Usually the view of incoming patients is limited to relevant personnel. However, other patients waiting in the emergency area are at times traumatized by the sight of terrible trauma to patients brought into the emergency room. Without training and primary and secondary prevention opportunities, these individuals are vulnerable to PTSD. In most emergency departments, injured patients now enter via the ambulance entrance and cannot be seen by other waiting patients.

Returning to the five people injured in the accident, hopefully they will be seen by a psychiatric consultant in the emergency department and referred to a secondary prevention program that involves debriefing as soon as possible, then individual, group, and family therapy as appropriate. These interventions are usually of brief duration, but needs must be individualized. As previously discussed, there can be great differences in reaction to a given trauma, depending on a number of variables.

We have reviewed an example of a small disaster, and the problems and needs of the different groups of people involved. The scope of this disaster does not require an overall disaster coordinator, since the trained groups of people know what to do and can communicate with one another directly and adequately as necessary.

A MEDIUM DISASTER

For a medium disaster,[15] I will use the example of a gunman shooting in a fairly large restaurant, since I was close to one not long ago. As the gunman kept shooting, injuring and killing people who were complete strangers to him, some people froze and were unable to move, while others sought escape. By the time the shooting stopped, there were people going in all directions, even through broken windows. Everyone who was not seriously injured went directly home. The various trained emergency units in the area responded promptly, coordinated their efforts, and all the seriously injured were rapidly evacuated to hospitals, some by medical unit helicopters from the nearby military base.

I was not personally aware of the levels of primary and secondary prevention of PTSD for the various medical units or for the involved police who were on the scene even before the shooting stopped. Hopefully, the prevention training was adequate. The medical and surgical problems were well handled, and we have already reviewed the needs of the various helping groups. I will therefore focus on the emotional and psychological issues.

Within hours, many community mental health professionals were volunteering to treat the victims of this disaster. The community response in general was excellent, but there were also problems. The mental health professionals did not know who to call to volunteer their services. Red Cross personnel tried to fill this gap. Salvation Army and other volunteer groups and individuals, as well as government agencies, also responded. However, nobody knew how many victims fled the restaurant with or without minor physical injuries. The local MHMR to its credit announced a meeting in a local hotel. However, that was a couple of days later, still time for debriefing to be helpful. Announcements on radio and TV advertised the meeting, but there was no way to know what percentage of victims would attend. Chances are that the ones who needed it most stayed home and never came forth.

I am describing some of the things that happened not to be critical but to make some helpful suggestions for dealing with such unanticipated emergencies. After something like this happens, it is always helpful to look back and think about constructive changes. I admire all those from the community and elsewhere, including mental health professionals, who quickly came forth to help. Nothing I say is intended as criticism for all that effort and caring. However, we must ask ourselves what we could have done better in order to learn for the future. We can work toward some ideal goals, recognizing that movement toward most goals must be gradual.

My first proposal involves the need for a mental health coordinator for all disasters who has expertise in the prevention and treatment of PTSD. The mental health coordinator could work with the medical coordinator who is responsible for coordinating the efforts of emergency medical teams and hospitals to expedite care and treatment for all those that are physically injured. Without such coordination, time and effort could be wasted. These things are also true for the mental health coordinator. The coordinators must be known to everyone concerned, and must be on the scene promptly to establish communication and coordination. This is now generally better accomplished by police and fire departments, for example, who have a coordinator on the scene promptly, and these coordinators maintain communication with one another and all units for best results.

Disaster drills held periodically are designed to improve disaster response through training and improved communication. However, I am not aware of disaster drills that involve a mental health coordinator, and I will focus on this position.

I think it would be helpful to designate individuals from the local medical society as mental health coordinators. They should be psychiatrists with knowledge and experience in the prevention and treatment of PTSD. Then everyone in the community knows where to turn and who to call when disaster strikes. More than one coordinator must be chosen, since one individual could be sick or away at the critical time. All inquiries about mental health issues could then be directed to the local medical society unless another number and location are selected and announced to the public.

In the restaurant shooting described, the mental health coordinator would suggest that the police stop all victims running from the restaurant so they can be taken to the selected meeting site for prompt debriefing. On the way the victim could be helped and encouraged by community volunteers who will also help them contact family members. Debriefing conducted by the mental health coordinator or designees is most helpful when done immediately after the trauma, and family members must be informed and involved as soon as possible. After this, victims and their families must be informed about individual, group, and family therapy meetings. The process is described under prevention of PTSD. Those designated by the mental health coordinator to supervise debriefing and subsequent treatment should also have knowledge and experience in the prevention and treatment of PTSD.

Following this particular disaster, prompt debriefing and plans for treatment of all victims to minimize the development of PTSD were not possible. There was no mechanism in place to accomplish that important process. Victims ran home and in some cases were afraid to leave the house for some time, so help was delayed or avoided. This caused them to suffer PTSD consequences that could have been reduced or avoided if prompt debriefing was available.

In addition to coordinating treatment plans, the mental health coordinator could advise involved individuals, groups, departments, and agencies in making all efforts most fruitful and effective. In contrast with a small disaster, the medium size disaster involves the coordination of many more individuals, groups, departments, and agencies that are responding.

The mental health coordinator also has some responsibility for those who were injured and taken to hospitals to be certain that they get debriefing and follow-up care. The hospital psychiatric consultant would most likely be contacted. After leaving the hospital, these individuals could join the program already in progress for those not physically injured, unless other suitable arrangements have been made. Since physical injury increases the possibility of developing PTSD, appropriate treatment is indicated to avoid the possibility of long term symptoms.

The mental health coordinator also has some responsibility for secondary prevention for emergency personnel that participated in various ways during the crisis and afterwards.[16] This includes volunteers from Red Cross and Salvation Army, as well as other individuals and organizations.[17] Some emergency units and organizations already have secondary prevention programs in place, but many do not. A therapeutic program should be available for all who were involved.

The mental health coordinator would have the additional responsibility of responding to disaster drills, and communicating with and educating all others involved about PTSD, such as police, firemen, and emergency medical crews. The coordinator could also advise these organizations or be a consultant for their primary and secondary PTSD prevention programs for employees. The coordinator could also recommend other qualified professionals for these responsibilities upon request. Reducing risks for PTSD for the many at risk people in these organizations and departments is important and worthwhile.

Another possible role for mental health coordinator would be coordination of the primary and secondary PTSD prevention programs for public agencies and private business. Here again the coordinator could supply a list of qualified professionals for any organization that wants to start or improve a program. Under prevention we reviewed the desirability of these programs for all organizations, particularly businesses or factories where there is greater risk of personal injury and disaster. With increasing violence and even shootings in public schools, I feel that primary prevention programs in schools would be important for both students and staff.

A LARGE (MAJOR) DISASTER

I will use the recent major hurricane in southern Florida as the example of a major disaster.[18] In that storm, most homes and buildings in the entire region were severely damaged or leveled, causing many injuries, and leaving thousands homeless. The injured were evacuated to hospitals fairly efficiently, often by helicopters that flew in from undamaged nearby areas. The entire population was traumatized by the fury of the storm, and then by the sight of their homes and communities completely destroyed.[19] Many were stripped entirely of earthly belongings, walked around stunned, and had difficulty mobilizing themselves to find food and shelter. They needed help. Local police, firemen, and emergency medical crews were likewise traumatized by the storm and extent of damage, but in most instances their training that included some primary prevention helped them keep functioning to meet the needs of the emergency. Nevertheless, many of them were affected by the sight of such terrible devastation.

It is immediately apparent that the many uninjured victims in the area needed lots of help from sources outside of their region.[20] Huge numbers of people needed clean drinking water and food, shelter, sanitation facilities, and many other physical needs. The response was national in scope. Individuals who lived close enough drove themselves into the damaged areas to help. Public and private agencies responded, including both state and federal agencies, also units from the armed forces who supplied food and water, built temporary housing, and helped care for medical and other needs. Most of the units and agencies had not previously communicated with one another during disaster drills, making communication and coordination more of a problem. Physicians from local areas also came in to help care for medical needs, but organizing such help was difficult. It was not long before outside people also came in to help rebuild roads and buildings, restore electricity, water supply, and communication.

The many people who came into the damaged areas to help usually had strong emotional reactions to the complete devastation they suddenly saw before them. Even some trained personnel had this problem, which could potentially result in PTSD. In other words, the helpers needed help to cope with this, but of course none was available. I am therefore describing not only a resident population at risk for developing PTSD, but also the many people who came in to help. We previously reviewed primary and secondary prevention for units like police, firemen, and emergency medical teams, and they will not be reviewed here. However, private citizens, those in Red Cross, Salvation Army, government agencies, and many other organizations involved in this major disaster probably did not have the benefit of such training. Without this training, vulnerability to PTSD is greater.

The dimensions of the management of PTSD in such a major disaster is much greater than in a medium disaster. I recall reading an article written by one of the psychiatrists from Miami who went into the devastated area on numerous occasions to help. He described his strong emotional reaction when first confronted by devastation on a scale he had never before seen. I think that most people in this situation question what one person can do, considering the scope of the problem.

Ideally in this type of disaster, it would be desirable to have debriefing as soon as possible for groups of thirty to fifty people, with subsequent individual, group, and family therapy. In addition to serving victims, qualified professionals should also offer primary and secondary prevention to police, firemen, emergency medical teams, and the many other volunteer units and groups and individuals working in the area. This would call for high level coordination of large numbers of qualified mental health professionals. I will offer some thoughts on this mighty challenge.

In discussing the medium disaster, I suggested a mental health coordinator from each county medical society. However, I think that major disasters also call for both national and state mental health coordinators. The national coordinator could come from The American Psychiatric Association or from the office of the Surgeon General, and state coordinators either from the state health department, state medical society, or the state psychiatric society. In the Florida disaster, for example, the national coordinator could have organized efforts from the federal government and other states, while the state coordinator would do the same for state aid. The state coordinator, for example, could keep county medical societies advised about needs, and individuals in the state who want to volunteer time would have a phone number to call. Instead of driving around and looking for an opportunity to be of service, the psychiatrist from Miami I mentioned earlier would have made a phone call and known right where to go to be of the greatest assistance.

Although I mentioned psychiatrists as coordinators, I also mentioned other mental health professionals with appropriate training and experience. The coordinator must designate leaders for various programs and therapies, and qualified psychologists and social workers could certainly share the responsibility for these programs.

Next, the question is where the national and state coordinators could find large numbers of qualified therapists. I feel that many qualified mental health professionals would volunteer time if there was some organization and structure, perhaps along the lines I have suggested. Direct appeals to psychiatry, psychology, and social service organizations would be one source. National coordinators could also work on creating a pool of qualified professionals from the armed services, Veterans Administration, and Public Health Service. State coordinators could maintain contact with county coordinators to appeal for volunteers, and could encourage the creation of a pool of qualified professionals from the state hospital system. In addition, there could be qualified professional trainees, such as psychiatric residents with the appropriate training and experience, who would also volunteer.

It is important to remember that PTSD can take a toll both physically and emotionally over a period of many years, causing suffering to patient and family, and resulting in multiple hospitalizations and office visits. Since many PTSD sufferers are no longer able to maintain employment, it changes tax payers into tax consumers. The national cost in human suffering, and also in dollars, of a major disaster is therefore huge and long term. Efforts to avoid or minimize PTSD in the ways described can greatly reduce the terrible cost.

SUMMARY OF RECOMMENDATIONS

PTSD exacts a high toll, both in terms of human suffering and financial cost, since PTSD is so common (even though it usually remains unrecognized). I therefore feel that comprehensive programs of primary and secondary prevention should become a national priority.

Programs must be considered at all levels: nationally, at state and community levels, and in businesses and schools of all sizes. Earlier in this chapter, I described how leadership responsibility for coping with disasters and for secondary prevention could be delegated through the appropriate national, state, and community medical societies. Specific programs for primary and secondary prevention have already been described (see Chap. 40). Implementing such programs would require a great deal of time, effort, and expense, but would be a worthwhile investment in the long run.

An essential element in approaching the broad problem would be public education, as well as education in specific programs, about the fact that each of us has feelings and emotional limits, and that it is possible for anyone to be overwhelmed enough to develop PTSD. The pressure for all of us to be tough and not let things bother us must be tempered with compassion and human understanding, so an individual need not feel ashamed of feeling fear in the face of trauma, nor of the symptoms that sometimes follow a particularly traumatic experience.

REFERENCES

1. Friedman M, Schneiderman C, West A: Measurement of combat exposure, post-traumatic stress disorder, and life stress among Vietnam combat veterans. *Am J Psychiatry 143:*537–539, 1986.

2. Kolb LC: The post-traumatic stress disorders of combat: a subgroup with a conditioned emotional response. *Milit Med 149:*237–243, 1984.

3. Kluznik J, Speed N, Van Valkenburg C, et al: 40-year follow-up of US prisoners of war. *Am J Psychiatry 143:*1443–1446, 1986.

4. Appelbaum PS, Jick RZ, Grisso T, et al: Use of posttraumatic stress disorder to support an insanity defense. *Am J Psychiatry 150:*229–234, 1993.

5. London DB, Zonana HV, Loeb R: Workers' compensation and psychiatric disability, in *Psychiatric Injury in the Workplace.* Edited by Larson R. Philadelphia, PA, Hanley and Belforth, 1988.

6. Resnick TJ: Malingering of post-traumatic stress disorders, in *Clinical Assessment of Malingering and Deception.* Edited by Rogers R. New York, Guilford, 1988.

7. Insanity Defense Work Group: American Psychiatric Association statement on the insanity defense. *Am J Psychiatry 140:*681–688, 1983.

8. Wilson JP, Zigelbaum SD: The Vietnam veteran on trial: the relation of post-traumatic stress disorder to criminal behavior. *Behavioral Science Law 1:*69–83, 1983.

9. Sparr LF, Atkinson RM: Post-traumatic stress disorder as an insanity defense: medicolegal quicksand. *Am J Psychiatry 143:*608–613, 1986.

10. Pitman RK, Orr SP, Forgue DF, Altman B, de Jong JB, Herz LR: Psychophysiologic responses to combat imagery of Vietnam veterans with posttraumatic stress disorder versus other anxiety disorders. *J Abnorm Psychol 99:*49–54, 1990.

11. Shalev AY, Orr SP, Pitman RK: Psychophysiologic assessment of traumatic imagery in Israeli civilian patients with posttraumatic stress disorder. *Am J Psychiatry 150:*620–624, 1993.

12. Orr SP, Claiborn JM, Altman B, Forgue DF, de Jong JB, Pitman RK, Herz LR: Psychometric profile of PTSD, anxious, and healthy Vietnam veterans: correlations with psychophysiologic responses. *J Consult Clin Psychol 58:*329–335, 1990.

13. Raphael B: *When Disaster Strikes.* New York, Basic Books, 1986.

14. Amick A, Kilpatrick D, Resnick H, et al: Public health implications of homi-

cide for surviving family members. Paper presented at the Society for Behavioral Medicine, San Francisco, CA, April 1989.

15. Smith EM, North CS: Aftermath of a disaster: Psychological response to the Indianapolis Ramada jet crash. *Quick Response Research Report #23.* Boulder, CO, Natural Hazards Research and Applications Information Center, 1988.

16. Raphael B: Rescue workers: stress and their management. *Emergency Response* 1:27–30, 1984.

17. Bartone P, Ursano R, Wright K, et al: The impact of a military air disaster on the health of assistance workers: a prospective study. *J Nerv Ment Dis* 177:317–328, 1989.

18. Madakasira S, O'Brien K: Acute post traumatic stress disorder in victims of a natural disaster. *J Nerv Ment Dis* 175:286–290, 1987.

19. Maida CA, Gordon NS, Steinberg A, et al: Psychosocial impact of disasters: Victims of the Baldwin Hills Fire. *Journal of Traumatic Stress* 2:37–48, 1989.

20. Shore JH, Tatum EL, Vollmer WM: Psychiatric reactions to disaster: the Mount St. Helen's experience. *Am J Psychiatry* 143:590–595, 1986.

INDEX